Days *of* Awe
and **Wonder**

Also by Marcus J. Borg

Days *of* Awe and **Wonder**

How to Be a **Christian** in the
Twenty-First Century

Marcus J. Borg

HarperOne
An Imprint of HarperCollinsPublishers

Pages 1–15, 45–63, and 89–110 from *Jesus: A New Vision* by Marcus
Borg. Copyright © 1987 by Marcus J. Borg. Courtesy of HarperCollins
Publishers.

Pages 27–43 from *Convictions: How I Learned What Matters Most* by
Marcus J. Borg. Copyright © 2014 by Marcus J. Borg. Courtesy of
HarperCollins Publishers.

Pages 139–48 from *The Christian Century,* August 28–September 4, 1985,
pp. 764–67. Copyright by The Christian Century Foundation; used by
permission. Current articles and subscription information can be found at
www.christiancentury.org. This material was prepared for Religion Online
by Ted and Winnie Brock.

HarperCollins books may be purchased for educational, business, or
sales promotional use. For information, please email the Special Markets
Department at SPsales@harpercollins.com.

FIRST EDITION

Designed by SBI Book Arts, LLC

Library of Congress Cataloging-in-Publication Data is available on request.

ISBN 978–0–06–245733–2

17 18 19 20 21 LSC/H 10 9 8 7 6 5 4 3 2 1

*In love for Marcus and dedicated
to the unending conversation*

*In gratitude for
Mickey Maudlin, Anna Paustenbach,
Mark Tauber, and Barbara Brown Taylor*

CONTENTS

Foreword

by Marianne Borg

For as long as there have been Christians, there has been considerable debate about what it means to be a Christian. From the authority of the Bible and the believability of its stories, to the meaning of Jesus, to what difference Christianity really makes, essential Christian ideas have evolved and been interpreted in various ways.

Yet the twenty-first century has seen even more dramatic change for Christianity. Old assumptions about and images of God no longer hold. Christianity is no longer considered essential for "salvation." It no longer provides an unambiguous moral compass. And the United States, "a Christian country," is now the most religiously diverse country in the world. As W. B. Yeats wrote in "Second Coming," we are in a post-Christian era; and what "rough beast, its hour come round at last, slouches towards Bethlehem to be born."

So just how important is Christianity to the twenty-first century? What does it mean to follow Jesus across terrain that is both trampled and uncharted? Does being Christian really matter anymore?

I suggest the angst among many Christians and the increasing number of "nones" on the religious affiliation line is good news. And it couldn't come at a more opportune time.

As poet Yehuda Amichai writes:

From the place where we are right
flowers will never grow
in the spring.
The place where we are right
is hard and trampled
like a yard,
but doubts and loves
dig up the world
like a mole, a plow.

Our doubts and loves are shaking our foundations, readying the ground for new life. Christianity is being born again.

Marcus Borg's journey reveals the fruit and labor of doubts and loves. In this collection of thoughts and ideas taken from a diversity of sources, from his dissertation written at age twenty-seven to his final book written at age seventy, you will find a companion for your doubts and loves. And you may just discover what it means to be a Christian in the twenty-first century.

A quick word about Marcus. Marcus was asked to preach on a Sunday morning as part of a lecture weekend. A children's sermon preceding Marcus's featured two darling dog puppets. To introduce Marcus to their young audience, one puppet exclaimed how excited he was to hear him speak. The other dog puppet paused and then shyly asked, "Who is Marcus Borg?"

Some of you know of Marcus Borg. Others of you are like the pup. Who is Marcus Borg? He is arguably one of the clearest, most accessible, insightful Jesus scholars and voices for Christianity in this century. He addressed many of our current questions and helped us fall in love with Christianity again, as if for the first time.

This volume is an opportunity to meet Marcus. For some, it will be a chance to read Marcus again as if for the first time, and for others it will truly be for the first time.

I want to identify a few themes that await you in this book. "The purpose of a book," suggests Thomas Merton, "is to teach you how to think and not to do your thinking for you. . . . As soon as any thought stimulates your mind or your heart, you can put the book down, because your meditation has begun." And, may I add, then pick this book up again. May it stimulate your mind and your heart.

First, there is a "more." Given all of life's ambiguities and the reality of impermanence and suffering, our existence is remarkable, wondrous. It evokes awe and amazement. We need to pay attention. Really pay attention. Lest we become blind to the awe and wonder that fills our days.

Second, Jesus is significant. Then and now. Because he is one of us. He is the embodiment of human possibility. He shows us our capacity for "knowing God," our capacity for courage, loving-kindness, and doing justice. This is hopeful.

Third, context matters. The first-century world was fraught with economic injustices, oppressive social and political structures, and claims of monopoly on God. Jesus was deeply affected and concerned about the sufferings and inequities of his day. So much so that he dedicated his entire life to the welfare of others. Jesus was equally concerned that we come to realize the nature of and the Reality that is God. In us. For us. Beyond us. Our lives depend upon it. How are we to respond to the complexities of the context of our lives? What is real? How, then, shall we live?

Fourth, there is "a way" of life that is sustainable. In brief, it is the way of compassion. Compassion is at the heart of all the great religious traditions. Each tradition is like a prism or a lens that gives us a distinctive perspective. We see only in part. Together we can find the way. The lens of Christianity, clarified and refracted in the work of these pages, is a way of seeing that commands compassion, love of this wondrous life and all humanity, of all things seen and unseen, and the unceasing work for peace and justice. Jesus has been described as the face of God turned toward us. We see not only God in his life and even death;

we see ourselves. We are given disclosures of "the way." A lot to ponder.

Every age should think of itself as the "axial age," the pivotal time. Ours is no exception. We have unprecedented realms of knowledge and information at our disposal, medical advances, scientific discoveries, including the ubiquitous neutrino, the superhero of the subatomic particle world that prefers matter over antimatter. This is hopeful. Ours is a time of awe and wonder of a magnitude not known before.

A cautionary note: we also have an unprecedented capacity for self-destruction, not only of humanity, but also of the planet. The stakes have never been higher. What we do now matters.

And here I return to Christianity. Why be a Christian in the twenty-first century? Because it gives us a vision. And a hope. And a way. The language of the New Testament talks about the "kingdom of God." Which is here, now. Which is what this world would be like if God was king and Caesar was not. The vision of Christianity for a just, sane, nonviolent world is not utopian. It is within our capacity. And such capacity requires that we take up the crucible of transformation. Transformation, individually and collectively, is the key ingredient for liberation. Without our participation in transformation and embodying lives of compassion, the kingdom of God will not come. It is up to us, and we are not alone.

This volume will explore these themes and others. May the discoveries here give us hope, like flowers in the spring that emerge from a season that looks to some like death. Marcus Borg's doubts and loves plowed ground. His life and work led him to rediscover the heart of Christianity. For himself, and for us. With new eyes and, yes, a new heart, being Christian in the twenty-first century can make the world a better place.

As a benediction, I close with this passage from the Jewish Sabbath Prayer Book:

> Days pass, and the years vanish, and we walk sightless among miracles. Fill our eyes with seeing and our minds with knowing. Let there be moments when your Presence, like lightning, illumines the darkness in which we walk. Help us to see, wherever we gaze, that the bush burns, unconsumed. And we, clay touched by God, will reach out for holiness and exclaim in wonder, "How filled with awe is this place . . ."

Marianne Borg
The Transfiguration
The Last Sunday in
Epiphany, 2017

Become part of the unending conversation.
The Marcus J. Borg Foundation, Inc.
www.marcusjborgfoundation.org

Days *of* Awe and **Wonder**

Chapter 1

Listening to the Spirit

WHEN I WAS A YOUNG TEACHER in my mid-twenties, an older colleague delighted in characterizing modern theology as "flat-tire" theology: "All of the *pneuma* has gone out of it." The irony of his comment depended on the double meaning of *pneuma,* a Greek word meaning both "air" and "spirit."[1] I understood his point, but I wasn't sure I agreed with it. For me, modern theology was a joy: insightful, challenging, liberating.

Though I still see modern theology as a treasure of great value for both church and culture, I also see that my colleague's statement was (and is) largely correct, not only

Originally published in *Jesus: A New Vision* (1987).

about theology in general, but also about biblical scholarship and historical Jesus studies in particular.[2] Within scholarly circles, Jesus's relationship to the world of Spirit is seldom taken seriously.[3] Attention is directed to what he *said,* and sometimes even to what he *did,* but seldom is attention paid to what he *was.*

What Jesus was, historically speaking, was a Spirit-filled person in the charismatic stream of Judaism. This is the key to understanding what he was like as a historical figure. In an important sense, all that he was, taught, and did flowed out of his own intimate experience of the "world of Spirit."

The "World of Spirit"

The notion of a "world of Spirit" is a vague and difficult notion in the contemporary world. By it I mean another dimension or layer or level of reality in addition to the visible world of our ordinary experience. This notion of "another world," understood as *actual* even though nonmaterial, is quite alien to the modern way of thinking. The modern worldview, or "picture of reality," sees reality as having essentially one dimension, the visible and material realm.[4] Deeply ingrained in all of us who have grown up in modern Western culture, this worldview makes us skeptical about another reality. For most contemporary people, believing in another reality requires "faith," understood as affirming that which on other grounds is doubtful.[5] The "world of Spirit" is not part of our taken-for-granted understanding of reality, not part of our worldview.

But the notion of another reality, a world of Spirit, was the common property of virtually every culture before ours, constituting what has been called the "primordial tradition."[6] Appearing in a multiplicity of cultural forms, indeed in virtually as many forms as there are cultures, it was almost a "cultural universal," the "human unanimity" prior to the modern period. Essential to it are two claims.

First, in addition to the visible material world disclosed to us by ordinary sense perception (and modern science), there is another level of reality, a second world of nonmaterial reality, charged with energy and power. This basic division of reality into two levels can be spoken of in many ways—as the sacred and the profane, the holy (or "numinous") and the mundane, God and "this world," and so forth.[7] What is most important is the notion of another level or levels of reality rather than any particular set of terms. Moreover, the "other world"—the world of Spirit—is seen as "more" real than "this world." Indeed, the "other reality" is the source or ground of "this world."

Second, and very important, the "other world" is not simply an article of belief, but an element of experience. That is, the notion of another reality does not have its origin in prescientific speculation about the origin of things, primal anxiety about death, or the need for protection, but is grounded in the religious experience of humankind.[8] It is not merely believed in, but *known*.

To put this second claim somewhat differently, the world of Spirit and the world of ordinary experience are seen as not completely separate, but as *intersecting* at a number of points.⁹ Many cultures speak of a particular place as the "navel of the earth," the umbilical cord connecting the two worlds.¹⁰ Some cultures speak of the two worlds intersecting in particular historical events. But it is especially in the experience of individuals that the "other world" is known. In every culture known to us, there are men and women who experience union or communion with the world of Spirit, either "entering" it or experiencing it coming upon them. Those who experience it frequently and vividly often become mediators between the two worlds in a variety of cultural forms: as healers, prophets, lawgivers, shamans, mystics. Such men and women are charismatics in the proper sense of the word: people who know the world of Spirit firsthand.

The Primordial Tradition in the Biblical Tradition

The cultural tradition in which Jesus lived took for granted the central claims of the primordial tradition: there are minimally two worlds, and the other world can be known. At the heart of the Jewish tradition, indeed constituting it, was Israel's story of the intersection between the world of Spirit and the world of ordinary experience. That is what Israel's scriptures were about. The Hebrew Bible is Israel's story of events that were seen as disclosures of Spirit, of people who were experienced as mediators of Spirit, of laws and prophetic utterances believed to have been given by the Spirit.

This multilayered picture of reality runs throughout the Bible. The opening verse of Genesis portrays the visible world as having its origin in Spirit, in God: "In the beginning God created the heavens and the earth." Importantly, Spirit is not seen as abstract and remote, as a hypothetical first cause.[11] Rather, the world of Spirit is seen as alive and "personal," populated by a variety of beings: angels, archangels, cherubim, seraphim. At its center (or height or depth) is God, often spoken of as personal: as father, mother, king, shepherd, lover. Nonanthropomorphic terms can also be used: fire, light, Spirit.

It is difficult to know how literally we should take this language. Language about the "other world" is necessarily metaphorical and analogical, simply because we must use language drawn from the visible world to try to speak of another world constituted by very different realities and energies. If anything is to be communicated at all, it must be by analogy to what we know in the ordinary world or in images drawn from the ordinary world. Thus God is *like* a father or mother, *like* a king, *like* a shepherd, *like* fire; but God is not *literally* any of these things. Yet, though the language is metaphorical, the realities are not.

Moreover, this other world is not *literally* somewhere else. It is not the localized heaven of the popular imagination. Though God can be spoken of as a being "up in heaven," the tradition makes it clear that God and the world of Spirit are not literally elsewhere. Rather, according to the tradition, God is everywhere present. To use somewhat technical but useful theological language, for the biblical tradition God is *immanent* (everywhere present, omnipresent), even as God is also *transcendent* (not to be identified with any particular thing, not even with the sum total of things). As omnipresent and immanent, God and the world of Spirit are all around us, including within us. Rather than God being somewhere else, we (and everything that is) are in God.[12] We live in Spirit, even though we are typically unaware of this reality.[13]

Biblical Mediators Between the Two Worlds

Israel affirmed that the world of Spirit was *known*. It intersected with "this world" at many points: historically, especially in the exodus and the return from exile, though also in other central events of its history; culticly, in the Temple in Jerusalem, which was seen as the navel of the earth connecting this world to the other world, which was its source; and personally, in the devotional and spiritual experiences of ordinary people and especially in Spirit-filled mediators such as Moses and the prophets. It is this tradition of Spirit-filled mediators that is most significant for understanding the historical Jesus.

From start to end, the Bible is dominated by such figures, beginning with the Genesis stories of the patriarchs, the "fathers" of Israel. Abraham saw visions and entertained heavenly visitors. Jacob had a vision of a fiery ladder connecting the two worlds, with angels ascending and descending on it. Afterwards he exclaimed, "This is the gate of heaven"—that is, the doorway into the other world (Gen. 28:17).[14] In the last book of the Bible, the vision of John begins with a similar image: "After this I looked, and there in heaven a door stood open!" (Rev. 4:1).[15] What is true of the beginning and end of the Bible is also true of its great figures throughout the tradition.

The first five books of the Bible (the Pentateuch) center on Moses, the main human figure of Israel's history, indeed its "founder." According to the brief obituary at the end of Deuteronomy, he knew God "face to face." According to Exodus, he repeatedly ascended the mountain of God (symbolizing the connection between the two worlds?) and there was given the words he imparted to his followers as "divine law." On one occasion after coming down from the mountain, we are told, his face actually glowed with the radiance of the holy, which he had encountered (Exod. 34:29–35). Throughout the Pentateuch, Moses functions as a mediator between the two worlds: as divine lawgiver, as channel of power from the world of Spirit, and as intercessor on behalf of his people (Exod. 32:7–14; Num. 14:13–19).

The experience of the other world and the role of mediation are also central to the prophets, including Elijah, as well as the classical prophets. Though a much more shadowy figure than Moses, Elijah was one of the central heroes of the Jewish tradition. Like Moses, he was frequently in the wilderness and sojourned to the sacred mountain, where he also experienced a theophany (an experience of God or "the holy"). Even as the stories about him emphasize the issues of social justice and loyalty to God that characterize the later prophets, he is also clearly portrayed as a "man of Spirit": he traveled "in the Spirit" and was a channel for the power of Spirit as both a healer and rainmaker. At the end of his life he was carried into the other world by "chariots of fire."[16]

One hundred years later, in the eighth century BCE, the mission of the prophet Isaiah began with an overwhelming experience of the other world:

> In the year that King Uzziah died, I saw the Lord sitting on a throne, high and lofty; and the hem of his robe filled the temple. Seraphs were in attendance above him; each had six wings: with two they covered their faces, and with two they covered their feet, and with two they flew. And one called to another and said: "Holy, holy, holy is the LORD of hosts; the whole earth is full of his glory." The pivots on the thresholds shook at the voices of those who called, and the house filled with smoke. (6:1–4)

In the Temple, the sacred place connecting the earth to the other realm, Isaiah momentarily "saw" into the other world: a vision of God upon the divine throne, surrounded by strange, unearthly six-winged creatures. But he did not simply "see" into the other world; he was, in a sense, *in it,* for he became a participant in the scene:

> Then one of the seraphs flew to me, holding a
> live coal that had been taken from the altar with
> a pair of tongs. The seraph touched my mouth
> with it and said: "Now that this has touched
> your lips, your guilt has departed and your sin is
> blotted out." (6:6–7)

The image of seeing into another world is also used to describe the origin of Ezekiel's mission as a prophet some 150 years later:

> In the thirtieth year, in the fourth month, on the
> fifth day of the month, as I was among the exiles
> by the river Chebar, *the heavens were opened, and
> I saw visions of God.* (1:1)

Alternatively, prophets spoke of the Spirit descending upon them: "The Spirit of the Lord *fell upon me*" (Ezek. 11:5); "The Spirit of the Lord God is *upon me*" (Isa. 61:1). The direct encounters with the world of Spirit reported by Isaiah and Ezekiel generally characterized the prophets. They spoke of knowing and being known by God, of seeing visions, of being present in the "heavenly council."[7]

In Jesus's day, the stream was not frozen in the past, but continued to flow. In the century before and after Jesus, the charismatic phenomenon continued in a number of Jewish "holy men" active primarily in Galilee.[18] Known for the directness of their relationship to God and the length and effectiveness of their prayer, they were delegates of their people to the other world, mediating the power of the Spirit especially as healers and rainmakers. The two most famous, Honi the Circle-Drawer and Hanina ben Dosa, were both compared to that earlier person of the Spirit, Elijah.

They had power over demons, who recognized and feared them. Among the healings credited to Hanina, active around the middle of the first century CE, one involved a cure from a distance. He healed the son of Rabbi Gamaliel who was mortally ill with a fever, despite the fact that Hanina was in Galilee and Gamaliel's son was in Jerusalem, some one hundred miles away.

These charismatics were known for their intimacy with God. Some were even heralded as "son of God" by a "heavenly voice": "The whole universe is sustained on account of *my son* Hanina."[19] The role of intercession characteristic of the Spirit-filled tradition appears in a saying attributed to Honi the Circle-Drawer (first century BCE), which also uses the language of sonship: "Lord of the universe, thy sons have turned to me because I am as a *son of the house* before thee."[20] As "son of the house," he was sought by the other "sons" as an intercessor with the world of Spirit.[21]

The most famous follower of Jesus in the generation after his death was also a Spirit-filled mediator. Near the middle of the first century the apostle Paul wrote about his own journey into the world of Spirit:

> I know a person in Christ [Paul is referring to
> himself] who fourteen years ago was caught up
> to the third heaven—whether in the body or out
> of the body I do not know; God knows. And
> I know that such a person—whether in the
> body or out of the body I do not know; God
> knows—was caught up into Paradise and heard
> things that are not to be told, that no mortal is
> permitted to repeat. (2 Cor. 12:2–4)[22]

Notable is the picture of reality as having several lay-
ers, the image of entering it, the uncertainty whether the
experience was "in the body" or out of it, the notion of
paradise as a realm that can be entered in the present,
and the ineffability of the other world, which is filled
with realities that cannot be adequately described in
language drawn from this world. Paul's conversion is
also best understood as a charismatic experience,[23] and
he was, according to Acts, a healer, a channel for power
from the world of Spirit.

Thus the stream in which Jesus stood, going back
through the prophets to the founder and fathers of Israel,
as well as the stream that issued forth from him, centered
on Spirit-filled mediators who bridged the two worlds.
The stream was the source of the tradition; its literature,
both the Hebrew Bible and the New Testament, clusters
around them. Indeed, in the specific sense of the term used
here, the heart of the biblical tradition is "charismatic," its
origin lying in the experience of Spirit-endowed people

who became radically open to the other world and whose gifts were extraordinary.

The Collision with Our Way of Seeing

Even people familiar with the Bible are often unaware how much the experience of the other world pervades it. Because the notion of another realm or dimension of reality and of people who can be mediators between the two worlds is alien to our way of seeing, we need to return to this theme as we draw this section to a close.

Those of us socialized in the modern world have grown up in a culture with a largely secularized and one-dimensional understanding of reality. Though remnants of a religious worldview remain, the dominant worldview in the modern period flows from the scientific and technological revolution of the last few centuries. For us, perceiving reality within the framework of this worldview, what is real is essentially the material, the visible world of time and space. What is real is ultimately made up of tiny bits and pieces of "stuff," all operating in accord with laws of cause and effect, which can be known. Reality is constituted by matter and energy interacting to form the visible world. In short, there is but one world.

As we grew up, the process of learning this worldview was largely unconscious. We were not directly instructed in the subject of "worldview," but it was the presupposition for all subjects. Moreover, we are not normally conscious of its presence or function within our minds. As a fundamental picture of reality, the modern worldview is like a map laid over reality, conditioning both our experience and understanding. We pay attention to what it says is real. The depth of this worldview in us, the taken-for-granted way in which it affects our understanding, is remarkable, even in people with a religious upbringing.[24]

This nonreligious one-dimensional understanding of reality makes the other world and the notion of mediation between the two worlds unreal to us. Though we may grant that unusual healings do occur, we are inclined to think that some psychosomatic explanation is possible. Though we grant that exceptional people may indeed enter a trancelike state and experience a journey into another world, we are inclined to view their experience of nonordinary reality as purely subjective, as an encounter with merely mental realities within the psyche or as hallucinations. To put it mildly, the "other world" is no longer taken for granted as an objectively real "other reality." Indeed, within the modern framework, frequent and vivid experiences of another reality mark a person as clinically psychotic.

Even biblical scholarship in the modern period has generally not known what to do with the category of "Spirit." Most biblical scholars work within the modern academy, whose canons of respectability include a methodology that assumes the truthfulness of the modern worldview. Typically spending eight or more years in college and graduate school and often remaining as teachers, we often measure our time in the academy in decades rather than years.

Texts that report "paranormal" happenings, whether they are visions of another realm or miracles, are either largely ignored or else interpreted in such a way that they do not violate our sense of what is possible or real.[25] Thus, because we do not know what to do with the world of Spirit, we tend not to give it a central place in our historical study of the biblical tradition.

But the reality of the other world deserves to be taken seriously. Intellectually and experientially, there is much to commend it. The primary intellectual objection to it flows from a rigid application of the modern worldview's definition of reality. Yet the modern view is but one of a large number of humanly constructed maps of reality. It is historically the most recent and impressive because of the degree of control it has given us; but it is no more an absolute map of reality than any of the previous maps. All are relative, products of particular histories and cultures; and the modern one, like its predecessors, will be superseded.

Already there are signs of its eclipse. Within the theoretical sciences, the modern worldview in its popular form has been abandoned.[26] At macro and micro levels, reality behaves in strange ways that stretch the popular worldview beyond its limits. The "old map" is being left behind. Of course, this does not prove the truth of the religious worldview, but it does undermine the central reason for rejecting it. The worldview that rejects or ignores the world of Spirit is not only relative, but is itself in the process of being rejected. The alternative to a one-dimensional understanding of reality can claim most of the history of human experience in its support. People throughout the centuries, in diverse cultures, regularly experienced another realm that seemed to them more real, powerful, and fundamental than the world of our ordinary experience. Not only is there no intellectual reason to suppose the second world to be unreal, but there is much experiential evidence to suggest its reality.[27]

In any case, quite apart from the question of ultimate truth, it is necessary to take seriously the reality of the world of Spirit if we wish to take the central figures of the Jewish tradition seriously. To try to understand the Jewish tradition and Jesus while simultaneously dismissing the notion of another world or immediately reducing it to a merely psychological realm is to fail to see the phenomena, to fail to take seriously what these charismatic mediators experienced and reported. For many of us, this will require a temporary suspension of our disbelief. Jesus's vivid experience of the reality of Spirit radically challenges our culture's way of seeing reality.

Chapter 2

Faith

A JOURNEY OF TRUST

IN THE TWELFTH CHAPTER OF GENESIS Abraham is called by God to leave his homeland on a journey to a land that he did not know. Abraham is promised that he will be the father of a great nation and have many descendants, descendants as numerous as the sands of the seashore and the stars of the sky. And of course, Abraham is one of the most central figures of our tradition. In a very important sense, he is our ancestor. He is the first historical figure

Sermon delivered at Calvary Episcopal Church, Memphis, Tennessee, as part of the Lenten Noonday Preaching Series, March 8, 2005.

mentioned in the pages of the Hebrew Bible. He is the father of the Jewish people and thus the father of the three great Abrahamic traditions: Judaism, Christianity, and Islam. We are all children and heirs of Abraham, and the promise of the text has thus been fulfilled. Abraham's descendants are as numerous as the stars of the sky and the sands of the seashore.

In this sermon I want to highlight two primary characteristics of Abraham in the Bible. Abraham was a person of faith who set out on a journey in response to a call, the prompting of the voice of God. These are the central images in my sermon today: *the Christian life as a journey and the role of faith in that life.* Today, I want to focus your attention on what Abraham's journey was like as a foray, a prototype of the journey of all of us.

So I turn to a *journey image* of the Christian life and what that might mean for us. Let me begin by noting that it's very different from the image of the Christian life with which I grew up. I grew up in the Lutheran Church, and I'm deeply grateful for my Lutheran heritage. But one of the consequences of that Lutheran upbringing is that I thought that being a Christian was primarily about believing—about believing in the Bible, believing in Jesus, believing in God, believing in the truth of the Christian tradition. Among the reasons I thought it was about believing was because of the primacy given to faith in the Lutheran tradition, which I understood to mean belief.

It's also because I grew up in the modern world, as all of us did, where many traditional Christian beliefs have been called into question by modern knowledge. Thus, I thought that the Christian life was about believing in a variety of things that didn't make a lot of sense, but that's what faith was all about. I think that's true not just for people who grew up as Lutherans, but for many modern Christians. Moreover, it isn't just that it was about believing, but it was about believing now for the sake of salvation later, for the sake of heaven later.

I now see the Christian life very differently. I now see it as a journey. Here I am using "journey" as a comprehensive metaphor or image for what the Christian life is like and most centrally about. This journey image is a very rich metaphor, and I invite you for a few minutes to think with me about some of the resonances of speaking of it as a journey. To be on a journey is to be in movement. Moving from place to place—there is change in such a life. A journey is a process that involves our whole being. It involves our feet as well as our minds and our heads. A journey involves following a path or a way. To be on a journey is not to be wandering aimlessly, though there may be times when it feels like that; people have gone on this journey before us, and there is a trail, a path, a way that we are called to. The journey image suggests that the Christian life is more like following a path than it is about believing things with our minds.

A journey also involves a leaving, a departing, a setting out. It involves leaving home. To go back to the Abraham story, Abraham was called to leave his homeland for a land that he did not know. Why did Abraham leave? Why was he willing to do that? Well, the texts in Genesis don't tell us the answer to that. So I'm going to follow an ancient rabbinic mode of interpretation and speculate when the text doesn't give us the information.

Again, I invite you to imagine with me the reasons why Abraham might have left a familiar place to begin on a journey that led he knew not where. What made him willing to leave? What was his life like that he was willing to listen to this voice that called him to go?

One possibility is that his old life had become dull. One ordinary day after another. Same ole, same ole. That feeling of measuring our life out in coffee spoons that the poet T. S. Eliot speaks about. Or perhaps his old life stank. Perhaps there was something rotten in Denmark in his own life or in the life of his society, and it smelled. Maybe it was more than just dull; perhaps Abraham felt as if he was caught in a cesspool. Or perhaps his old life was oppressive, constrained, hemmed in. Perhaps it was filled with unnecessary social misery. Maybe he felt so hemmed in that sometimes he couldn't even breathe. Or perhaps his old life was filled with yearning, with an ache for something more. Yearning for another land, another way of being. That feeling of perhaps being full, but still hungry.

Whatever his reasons, the journey image suggests for us that the Christian life involves leaving an old way of being. And for us Christians, that journey has a direction, and essential biblical stories and themes of scripture powerfully suggest what that direction is. If we take the exodus story as an indicator of that journey, it's a journey that leads from bondage to liberation. Or if we take the Jewish experience of exile in Babylon as the paradigm for the journey's story, it is a journey that leads from exile and alienation to return and homecoming, from seeing ourselves as being of little or no account to seeing ourselves as the beloved of God. Or to use the sight and light metaphors that run through scripture, a journey that leads from blindness to sight, from being in the dark to being in the light. Or it's a journey that leads from convention to compassion, from living our lives in accord with conventional values to living our lives in accord with the central biblical values of compassion and justice.

All of this is where our journey leads. The central quality of Abraham's journey and of our own journey is that *it involves faith*. Abraham, in that great eleventh chapter of the Letter to the Hebrews in the New Testament, is one of the heroes of faith; in fact, more verses in that chapter are spent speaking about Abraham as a hero of faith than about anybody else. Abraham is not only a person who goes on a journey; he's a person of faith. That's the second thing I wanted to speak about in this sermon. What is faith? How are we to understand it?

Let me begin with a quick little parenthetical remark about the etymology or origin of the Hebrew word for "faith." The Hebrew word for faith in the Old Testament is *emunah*. What makes that word interesting is that it's the sound that a baby donkey makes when it is calling for its mother. To appreciate that, you have to say *emunah* so it sounds like that. If you want to hear the meaning of *emunah*, you need to say it like soft braying. The point is that faith in the Hebrew Bible is like a baby donkey calling or crying out for its mother. There's something kind of wonderful about that. There is an element—I don't know if you want to say of desperation in it or not, but there certainly is an element of confidence also that the cry will be heard.

Faith has come to have four meanings in the Christian tradition. The first of these four is, I am convinced, a modern distortion, even as it is probably the most common meaning on the popular level. The other three are ancient and traditional and wonderfully complementary. You can have them all, but let me begin with the modern distortion.

The modern distortion of faith is the one I learned growing up around the middle of this century: faith as believing. Faith as believing the doctrines of the Christian tradition, faith as believing that there is a God, faith as believing that Jesus is divine, faith as believing that Jesus died for your sins—in short, faith as believing certain statements to be true.

There are a number of reasons why I say that's a modern distortion. First of all, try to imagine what faith was like before the Enlightenment, that great period of Western history that began in the seventeenth or eighteenth century. Prior to the Enlightenment, in the Christian culture of the Reformation, the Middle Ages, and earlier, nobody had any trouble believing that the Bible came from God, that the Genesis stories of creation were true, that Jesus walked on water, and so forth. It didn't take faith to believe any of that; that was simply part of the taken-for-granted understanding of people living in Western Christendom. It's only when those things started to be questioned that suddenly faith came to mean believing what otherwise doesn't make a lot of sense to you. And faith came to mean what Bishop Robinson called it some thirty-five years ago: believing forty-nine impossible things before breakfast.

Now, I don't want simply to knock that, because for many people that's been a way of holding on to the meaningfulness of the Christian tradition when it seems to have been radically questioned. But I also want to say that faith as believing the right things is not only a modern distortion, but in many ways it is absolutely impotent in our lives. You can believe all the right things and still be a jerk. You can believe all the right things and still be miserable. Faith as believing, that is, believing with our head, is really pretty impotent. So let me turn to the three more ancient and authentic meanings of faith.

In each case, I'm going to speak about the meaning of the word "faith," but also about its opposite, because I think that sometimes we get clarity about the meaning of a word by considering what its opposite is. With the first meaning of faith I spoke about, the opposite of faith as belief is, of course, doubt or disbelief. I can recall as an adolescent finding my embryonic doubts moving toward disbelief. I thought they were sinful, because I thought it was the opposite of what God wanted from me.

To turn now to the other three, the first of these three has a Latin name. I'm going to use the Latin name both to suggest the antiquity of the notion, but also because I think it's a way of understanding what faith means in this case. The first of these last three is faith as *fiducia*. We get the word "fiduciary" from it. This is basically faith as trust, faith as radical trust in God, which can go along with great uncertainty about beliefs. The opposite of faith as trust is not doubt. The opposite of faith as trust is anxiety. You can measure the amount of faith as trust in your life by the amount of anxiety you have in your life. I mention that not to give you one more thing to beat yourself up about, but to suggest that perfect faith as trust casts out anxiety. Think of how wonderful it would be to live your life without anxiety. The journey of faith that leads to greater trust can cast anxiety out and free us from that self-preoccupying force.

The second of the ancient and authentic meanings of faith is *fidelitas* in Latin. The English, of course, is "fidelity." This is faith as fidelity to a relationship, fidelity to the relationship with God, in other words faithfulness. Again, it has very little to do with what we believe with our heads; it's faithfulness to that relationship. The opposite of faith as fidelity is not, once again, doubt. It is, to say the obvious, infidelity, unfaithfulness. In the biblical tradition, this was frequently referred to as adultery. When the prophets rail against adultery, they're not talking about sexual behavior. They're using a sexual metaphor as a way of talking about unfaithfulness to God. And yet another word for infidelity in the biblical tradition is idolatry, namely, to be faithful to something other than God.

The third and final of these more ancient and authentic ways of understanding faith—I don't have a Latin word here—is faith as a way of seeing and, in particular, faith as a way of seeing the whole, the whole of that in which we live and move and have our being. I'm going to exposit this briefly in language that we owe to the great American theologian H. Richard Niebuhr, who points out that there are three different attitudes we can take toward the whole—three different ways we can see the whole.

One way we can see the whole of what is is as hostile toward us, threatening toward us in severe form. Of course, this is paranoia. But there are much milder forms of this; indeed, popular-level Christianity might even see things this way. God is seen as the one who is going to get us unless we offer the right sacrifice, have the right beliefs, and so on. But even apart from a religious context, if you see reality as threatening or hostile, and it's easy to see it that way—"The bottom line is it is going to get us all; we're all going to die"—then your response is likely to be one of self-protection in various ways. You will try to find security against the devouring power that will consume us all.

A second way we can see the whole is as indifferent toward human existence, indifferent toward us. This is the understanding that emerges within the modern worldview, where all is seen as a meaningless collocation of atoms interacting with each other. If we see reality as indifferent to us, again the appropriate and most likely response is to try to build systems of security that will give us some meaning in the face of this radical insecurity. But again, the attention focuses upon the self and its well-being.

The third and final way that Niebuhr says we can see reality is to see the whole as gracious, nourishing, and supportive of life, to see it as that which has brought us into existence and continues to nourish us. There is nothing Pollyanna-ish about this. This attitude is still very much aware that the flower fades, the grass withers, that we all die. But to see reality as supportive, gracious, and nourishing creates the possibility of responding to life in a posture of trust and gratitude. And we're back to faith as trust.

Faith is thus about setting out on a journey like Abraham's in a posture of trust, seeking to be faithful to the relationship we are called into. We are invited to make that journey, that journey of faith, in which we learn to trust our relationship to God, learn to be faithful to that relationship, and learn to see in a new way. We will be led in that journey into an ever more wondrous and compassionate understanding of our lives with God. Indeed, if this is not what life is about, namely, growth and wonder and compassion, then I don't know what it is about.

The story of Abraham leads us to that marvelous question asked by the contemporary poet Mary Oliver. The question is, "What are you going to do with your one wild and precious life?" Are we going to remain in the world of the dull, the repetitive, the same ole, same ole, or are we, like Abraham, going to respond to that voice that invites us to leave our old way of being and enter a life beyond convention and our domestications of reality? The voice speaks of promise to us. "I will show you a better way, a better country."

Chapter 3

My Conversion to Mysticism

M Y THIRD CONVERSION was a series of experiences that began in my early thirties. They weren't the product of thinking, even though over time they have greatly affected my thinking, perhaps more than anything else has. And they made God real to me.

In retrospect, I understand that they were mystical experiences (more about that soon). But I did not know that at the time. I knew nothing about mysticism. It had not been part of four years of undergraduate and five years of graduate study in religion. Whenever I had tried to read books about mysticism on my own, they were utterly

Originally published in *Convictions* (2014).

opaque. My eyes glazed over. I couldn't figure out what they were talking about.

The experiences were brief: none lasted longer than a minute or so, and some only a few seconds. They may not sound like much as I describe them, but I have since learned that this is one of the classic features of experiences like these: they are difficult to express in words. Even when words can convey what was experienced, they can only inadequately convey how it was experienced and the transformative power of the experience.

Aware of that difficulty, I share one of these experiences that illustrates features common to all of them. It happened as I was driving through a sunlit rural Minnesota winter landscape alone in a nine-year-old MG two-seater roadster. The only sounds were the drone of the car and the wind through the thin canvas top. I had been on the road for about three hours when I entered a series of S-curves. The light suddenly changed. It became yellowy and golden, and it suffused everything I saw: the snow-covered fields to left and right, the trees bordering the fields, the yellow and black road signs, the highway itself. Everything glowed. Everything looked wondrous. I was amazed. I had never experienced anything like that before—unless perhaps in very early childhood, and so I no longer remembered it.

At the same time, I felt a falling away of the subject-object distinction of ordinary everyday consciousness—that "dome" of consciousness in which we experience ourselves as "in here" and the world as "out there." I became aware not just intellectually but experientially of the connectedness of everything. I "saw" the connectedness, experienced it. My sense of being "in here" while the world was "out there" momentarily disappeared.

That experience lasted for maybe a minute and then faded. But it had been the richest minute of my life. It was not only full of wonder but also filled with a strong sense of knowing—of seeing more clearly and truly than I ever had. For about two years, I experienced more moments like this one. Some were just as vivid, and others were mere glimmerings. Most were visual. A few were triggered by music—a chamber orchestra in a college chapel, a symphony orchestra in a concert hall. The latter were not about a change in seeing, but about a change in hearing that again involved a falling away of the subject-object distinction of ordinary consciousness. During the experience, it was not I listening to the music but something outside myself. Only the music was left.

For about twenty years, I didn't have any more experiences like those, even as I yearned for them. I occasionally wondered why they had stopped and concluded that perhaps they had been for a season and had served their purpose. But what I had known in those experiences had changed me.

Then, in my mid-fifties, I had the longest and most intense such experience I've ever had. It happened an hour or two into a flight from Tel Aviv to New York—in economy class—a detail I add not to establish virtue, but to make it clear that I hadn't had any before-dinner drinks. I think the experience lasted about forty minutes—not that I timed it, but it began before dinner was served and ended as the flight attendants were removing the dinner service.

As during the experiences of my thirties, the light changed. It became golden. I looked around, and everything was filled with exquisite beauty—the texture of the fabric on the back of the seat in front of me, the tray full of food when it arrived (which I did not eat). Everybody looked beautiful—even a passenger who, as we left Tel Aviv, had struck me as perhaps the ugliest person I had ever seen. He had been pacing the aisle and was so hard to look at that I averted my eyes each time he passed by. Even he looked wondrous. My face was wet with tears. I was filled with joy. I felt that I could live in that state of consciousness forever and it would never grow old. Everything was glorious, filled with glory.

Back to my thirties: soon after these experiences began, a new teaching appointment required that I become familiar with mysticism in Christianity and other religions. That's when I realized that these were mystical experiences. Especially important was William James's classic book *The Varieties of Religious Experience,* published more than a century ago, still in print, and named by a panel of experts in 1999 as the second most important nonfiction book published in English in the twentieth century. The book combines the elements that made up James himself: a psychologist fascinated by the varieties of human consciousness and a philosopher pondering what all of this might mean.

Part of his book is about mystical experiences. Based on James's study of accounts of such experiences, he concluded that their two primary features are "illumination" and "union." Illumination has a twofold meaning. The experiences often involve light, luminosity, radiance. Moreover, they involve "enlightenment," a new way of seeing. "Union" (or "communion") refers to the experience of connectedness and the disappearance or softening of the distinction between self and world.

In addition, James names four other common features:

- *Ineffability:* The experiences are difficult, even impossible, to express in words. Yet those who have such experiences often try, usually preceded by, "It's really hard to describe, but it was like . . ."

- *Transiency:* They are usually brief; they come and then go.

- *Passivity:* One cannot make them happen through active effort. They come upon one—one receives them.

- *Noetic quality:* They include a vivid sense of knowing (and not just intense feelings of joy, wonder, amazement)—a nonverbal, nonlinguistic way of knowing marked by a strong sense of seeing more clearly and certainly than one ever has. What is known is "the way things are" when all of our language falls away and we see "what is" without the domestication created by our words and categories.

This way of knowing might be called direct cognition, a way of knowing not mediated through language.

Reading James and other writers on mysticism was amazing. In colloquial language, I was blown away. I found my experiences described with great precision. Suddenly, I had a way of naming and understanding them. Moreover, they were linked to the experiences of many people. They are a mode of human consciousness. They happen. And they are noetic: something is known that one did not know before.

I also learned other ways they have been named. Rudolf Otto (1869–1937) called them experiences of "the numinous," that which is behind and sometimes shines through our experience of phenomena. Abraham Heschel (1907–72) called them moments of "radical amazement," when our domestication of reality with language falls away and we experience "what is." Martin Buber (1878–1965) spoke of them as "I-Thou" or "I-You" moments in which we encounter "what is" as a "you" rather than as an "it," or an object. Abraham Maslow (1908–70) called them "peak experiences" that involve "cognition of being"—knowing the way things are. Mircea Eliade (1907–86), one of the most influential twentieth-century scholars of comparative religions, called them experiences of "the golden world," referring to their luminosity. Others have referred to them as moments of "unitive consciousness" and "cosmic consciousness."

Mystical Experiences and God

I learned one more thing as I read about mystical experiences; namely, people who had them most often spoke of them as experiences of God, the sacred, the Mystery with a capital *M* that is beyond all words. It had never occurred to me that what we call "God" could be experienced. For me, the word had referred to a being who might or might not exist, in whom one could believe or disbelieve, or about whom one could remain uncertain. But I realized there is a cloud of witnesses, Christian and non-Christian, for whom God, the sacred, is real, an element of experience, not a hypothetical being who may or may not exist and whom we can only believe in.

For the first time in my life, I understood the affirmation that the earth is full of "the glory of God." Perhaps the most familiar biblical example is in the prophet Isaiah. As he has a mystical experience of God, he hears the words, "Holy, holy, holy is the LORD of hosts; / the whole earth is full of his glory" (6:3). It is also familiar to Christians in liturgical churches in the Sanctus: "Holy, holy, holy Lord, God of power and might; heaven and earth are full of your glory." "Glory" in the Bible most often means radiance, luminosity. To affirm that heaven and earth (all that is) are full of God's glory means that everything is filled with the radiant luminosity of God. God, the sacred, pervades all that is, even though we do not often see it.

But there are moments in which our eyes are opened and we see the glory. Such a moment occurs in the climax of the book of Job. Throughout the book, Job questions the reality of God that he had learned, a God who rewarded the righteous and punished the wicked. Then, in the closing chapters of the book (38–41), Job experiences a magnificent display of the wonders of the universe. In the final chapter, he exclaims, "I had heard of you by the hearing of the ear—but now my eye sees you" (42:5). Job experienced the glory of God in the created world—and it changed his convictions about God. Believing or not believing in a concept of God was no longer an issue. Job learned that God, the sacred, *is,* and that God, the sacred, is both more than and other than Job had imagined.

Naming what is experienced in mystical experiences is difficult. People who have them not only consistently speak of them as ineffable, but as "unnamable," beyond all names. So it is in the story of the call of Moses in the book of Exodus. He sees a bush filled with fire and light yet not consumed, radiant with glory. A voice speaks to him, and Moses asks, "What is your name?" The response is a tautology: "I am who I am" (3:13–14). A tautology says nothing: it offers no information, but simply repeats itself. In Judaism, the most sacred name of God—so sacred that it may not even be pronounced—comes from this story. God, the sacred, is beyond all names—is "am-ness."

The most abstract and generic terms for what is experienced include "reality itself," "ultimate reality," or "Reality" with a capital *R*, "what is" when all our words fall away, or "is-ness without limits"—without the limits created by our language and categories. Buddhists sometimes speak of it as "suchness"—the way things are before our categorizations. William James called it "a more," a stupendous wondrous "more" that is more than what we had imagined even as it also is present everywhere and capable of being experienced anywhere.

In the religious traditions, this "more" is commonly named with the language of the tradition: as God, Lord, Allah, Brahman, Atman, and so forth. When French philosopher Blaise Pascal (1623–62) had a mystical experience of a fiery cross in 1654, he exclaimed, "God of Abraham, Isaac, and Jacob." We name and talk about mystical experiences with the language we know.

My experiences changed my sense of what is real. Like many people who grew up in modern Western culture, I had absorbed a way of seeing what is real that defined reality as the space-time world of matter and energy. That is the modern scientific worldview as most often understood at the popular level. What is real are those things we can observe and analyze through the methods of modern science. In retrospect, I understand that that worldview was primarily responsible for my adolescent and young adult doubts and skepticism about the reality of God, the sacred.

How Mystical Experiences Affected
My Understanding of God

The contrast to the concept of God I absorbed as I grew up is dramatic. Sometime in childhood, I began to think of the word "God" within the framework of "supernatural theism." Namely, "God" referred to a supernatural being separate and distinct from the universe, a supreme being who had created the universe a long time ago. In addition to being the creator, God was also the supreme authority figure who had revealed how we should live and what we should believe.

Supernatural theism and parental imagery for God, especially as "Father," often go together, producing what might be called "parent theism." The imagery of God as parent is rich. It suggests a relationship of intimacy, dependence, and protection. Our parents, if we had good parents, loved us and took care of us when we were little. Considerable evidence shows that most of us have a deep desire, sometimes unconscious, for a cosmic parent who will take care of us as our parents did when we were infants and toddlers and children. Or, if we had negligent parents, we want a parent who will take care of us better than our parents did.

Parent theism, especially God as "Father," also creates an image of God as the authoritarian parent: the rule giver and disciplinarian, the lawgiver and enforcer. This is "the finger-shaking God" whom we disappoint again and again. It is the God whose demands for obedience were satisfied by Jesus's death in our place.

The God of supernatural and parent theism is the God about whom I had become doubtful and anxious during my teens, agnostic during my college years, and then more and more atheist during my twenties. It became increasingly difficult and finally impossible for me to imagine that such a being existed.

The Alternative to Supernatural Theism

Mystical experiences change the question of whether God exists. To say the obvious, "is-ness," or "what is," *is.* It exists. What would it mean to argue about whether "is-ness" is? The question of God's existence is no longer about whether there is another being in addition to the universe. Rather, the question becomes: What is "is-ness"? What is "what is"? What is reality? Is it simply the space-time world of matter and energy as disclosed by ordinary sense perception and contemporary science? Or is it suffused by a "more," a radiant and glorious more?

A theology that takes mystical experiences seriously leads to a very different understanding of the referent of the word "God." The word no longer refers to a being separate from the universe, but to a reality, a "more," a radiant and luminous presence that permeates everything that is. This way of thinking about God is now most often called "panentheism." Though the word is modern, only about two centuries old, it names a very ancient as well as biblical way of thinking about God.

Its Greek roots indicate its meaning: the first syllable, *pan,* means "everything." The middle syllable, *en,* means "in." "Theism," comes from *theos,* the Greek word for "God," the sacred. Simply and compactly, "panentheism" means "everything is in God." The universe—everything that is—is in God, even as God is "more" than the universe.

Though panentheism is unfamiliar to many Christians, especially to those who know only supernatural theism, it is foundational to biblical ways of speaking about God. Its most concise crystallization is in words attributed to Paul in Acts: God "is not far from each one of us. For 'In God we live and move and have our being'" (17:27–28). Where are we in relationship to God? We live in God, move in God, have our being in God. God is not somewhere else, but all around us. We and everything that is are in God like fish are in water.

So also familiar language from Psalm 139 affirms. The psalmist asks: "Where can I go from your spirit? / Or where can I flee from your presence?"

If I ascend to heaven, you are there;
if I make my bed in Sheol, you are there.
If I take the wings of the morning
and settle at the farthest limits of the sea,
even there your hand shall lead me,
and your right hand shall hold me fast. (139:7–10)

The language reflects the three-story universe of the ancient imagination: whether one journeys to heaven above, descends to Sheol below, or travels to the limits of the sea, God is there. There is nowhere one can be and be outside of God—because God is everywhere.

These are not isolated examples. Though the Bible often personifies God as if God were a being separate from the universe, it also affirms that God is more than that. As King Solomon dedicated the Temple he built in Jerusalem to be God's dwelling place on earth, he asked, "But will God indeed dwell on the earth?" The text continues, "Even heaven and the highest heaven cannot contain you, much less this house that I have built!" (1 Kings 8:27).

To use semitechnical language from the history of theology, panentheism combines the transcendence and immanence of God. "Transcendence" refers to the "moreness" of God—God is more than the space-time universe of matter and energy. "Immanence" (from a root meaning "to dwell within") refers to the presence of God everywhere. Christian theologians since antiquity have affirmed both.

Most of us heard about both the transcendence and immanence of God as we were growing up, even though we may never have heard those words. We learned, in the opening words of the Lord's Prayer, that God is "in heaven." But we also learned that God is everywhere—that is, omnipresent. When one combines the two, the result is panentheism. It is orthodox Christian theology.

But supernatural theism, especially since the 1600s, has dominated popular Christianity. The belief that there is a parentlike all-powerful being who can protect and rescue us has always been attractive—even as it can be terrifying when God's wrath is emphasized. But in the 1600s, something new happened; namely, the birth of modern ways of knowing essentially removed the sacred from the world. What happened has been called "the disenchantment of nature": God, the sacred, was removed from the world. It has also been called "the domestication of transcendence," namely, the notion that the word "God" refers only to transcendence.

Supernatural theism has affected intellectuals as well. About a decade ago, I was one of several lecturers at a symposium called "Nature and the Sacred." The others included a Native American, a Buddhist, a Muslim, and a couple of nature philosophers. All of us were published authors and well known in our fields. About half described themselves as atheists. But all of us spoke about experiences of wonder. It became clear that we had all had mystical experiences of radical amazement.

But we were divided about God. Our division flowed from different understandings of the word. For the nontheists, "God" referred to the God of supernatural theism: the God I stopped believing in sometime during my twenties, the God critiqued in recent bestsellers on atheism, the God some of my students had in mind when they told me that they didn't believe in God. I learned many years ago to respond, "Tell me about the God you don't believe in." It was always the God of supernatural theism.

My religious experiences and conversion also affected my intellectual convictions. I have already mentioned two: they made God real to me, and they changed my understanding of the word "God."

But there is a third: I am convinced that there are no intrinsic conflicts between the intellect and Christianity, reason and religion. When there are, they are the unnecessary product either of a misunderstanding of religion and its absolutization or of the absolutization of a nonreligious worldview. Often both: most of today's "New Atheists" contrast the least thoughtful forms of religion with their robust confidence that contemporary science has the ultimate word on what is real.

And there is a fourth: being Christian is not about getting our intellectual beliefs, our theology, right. I emphasize this because much of this book is about a different understanding of Christianity, a change in how we think about God, the Bible, Jesus, and so forth. But being Christian is not having an intellectually correct theology.

There have been millions of "simple" Christians throughout the centuries. I do not mean "simpleminded" in a pejorative sense; I mean the people for whom the life of the mind was not central to their Christian lives. They were neither preoccupied with correct beliefs nor bothered by intellectual issues. Instead, Christianity was about loving

God and Jesus and seeking to love one another. Many of the saints were "simple" Christians in this sense.

Thus Christianity is not about getting our theology right. Theology is the intellectual stream of Christianity. In its narrow sense, it refers to an intellectual discipline that has been practiced by theologians from the earliest centuries of Christianity: the thoughtful articulation of what it means to be Christian.

Theological controversies over the centuries have sometimes been treated as if they were really important even though they were also often arcane. For instance, a trinitarian conflict split the Western and Eastern churches in 1054: Does the Holy Spirit proceed from the Father and the Son, or from the Father only? In the 1600s, "supralapsarianism" versus "infralapsarianism" almost divided the Reformed tradition. At issue was whether God decided to send a messiah (Jesus) before the first sin (because God knew it would happen) or only after it had happened (because only then was it necessary). More familiarly: infant baptism or adult baptism? Christians have often thought it is important to believe the right things.

In a broader sense, theology refers to "what Christians think." In this sense, all Christians have a theology—a basic, even if often simple, understanding—whether they are aware of it or not. In this broader sense, theology does matter. There is "bad" theology, by which I mean an understanding of Christianity that is seriously misleading, with unfortunate and sometimes cruel consequences. But the task of theology is not primarily to construct an intellectually satisfying set of correct beliefs. Its task is more modest. Part of its purpose is negative: to undermine beliefs that get in the way of taking Christianity seriously. Part of its purpose is positive: to construct a persuasive and compelling vision of the Christian life. But being Christian isn't primarily about having a correct theology by getting our beliefs right. It is about a deepening relationship with God as known especially in Jesus.

To return to mystical experiences, these episodes of sheer wonder, radical amazement, radiant luminosity often evoke the exclamation, "Oh my God!" So it has been for me, and for me that exclamation expresses truth. It is the central conviction that has shaped my Christian journey ever since. God is real, "the more" in whom we live and move and have our being.

It has also shaped my understanding of religions in general and major religious figures, including the central figures of the biblical tradition: Moses, the prophets, Jesus, Paul, and others. They were all people for whom God, the sacred, the more, was an experiential reality. That is where their way of seeing—their wisdom, their passion, and their courage—came from. They didn't simply believe strongly in God; they *knew* God. The central convictions and foundations of this book are that God is real and that the Bible and Christianity are the Christian story of our relationship with God, "the more," "what is."

Chapter 4

Jesus, Our Model for Being Spirit-Filled

GIVEN THE HISTORICAL IMPORTANCE of Jesus, it is re-markable that his public activity was so brief. The synoptic Gospels (Matthew, Mark, and Luke) imply that his ministry lasted only a year, the Gospel of John that it lasted three years or a bit more. Which is correct we can no longer know, but both agree that it was brief, extraordinarily so. The Buddha taught for forty-five years after his enlightenment, Muhammad for about twenty years. According to Jewish tradition, Moses led his people for

Originally published in *Jesus: A New Vision* (1987).

forty years. But Jesus's ministry was brief, a light flashing momentarily but brilliantly like a meteor in the night sky. What was he like?

Jesus was born sometime during the waning years of Herod the Great, who died in 4 BCE. Nothing is known about his life prior to the beginning of his ministry as a mature adult, except by inference.[1] He grew up in Nazareth, a hill town in the northern province of Galilee, some twenty miles inland from the Mediterranean Sea, fifteen miles from the Sea of Galilee to the east, and roughly one hundred miles north of Jerusalem. Most of his neighbors would have been farmers who lived in the village and worked the fields nearby or workers in the relatively small number of trades necessary to support agricultural life. He may or may not have been a carpenter; both "carpenter" and "carpenter's son" were used metaphorically within Judaism to mean "scholar" or "teacher."[2]

We may surmise that he experienced the socialization of a typical boy in that culture. Growing up in a Jewish home, most likely he attended school from roughly age six to at least twelve or thirteen, as a system of "elementary education" was widespread in Palestinian Judaism. His "primer" would have been the book of Leviticus. Whether he had formal training as a teacher of the Torah[3] beyond the schooling given to every boy, we do not know.

As a boy and young man, Jesus almost certainly attended the synagogue (a place of scripture reading and prayer in local communities) every Sabbath, and perhaps on Mondays and Thursdays as well. As a faithful Jew, he would have recited the *Shema* upon rising and retiring each day, the heart of which affirmed: "Hear, O Israel: The LORD is our God, the LORD alone. You shall love the LORD your God with all your heart, and with all your soul, and with all your might" (Deut. 6:4–5).[4] Presumably, he participated in the Jewish festivals and went on pilgrimages to Jerusalem. From the Gospels, it is clear that he was very familiar with his scriptures, the Hebrew Bible. He may have known it from memory, a feat not uncommon among the learned. The Psalms were probably his "prayer book."

That is about all we can know about Jesus prior to his emergence as a public figure, despite attempts to fill in the missing years in later apocryphal Gospels and occasional scholarly speculations. Suggestions that Jesus lived among the Essenes,[5] studied in Egypt, traveled to India, or somehow came in contact with the teachings of the Buddha are not only without historical foundation, but also unnecessary. We need not go beyond the mainstream of the Jewish tradition to find a "home" for everything that is said about him.

The Source of Jesus's Ministry: The Descent of the Spirit

When Jesus does appear on the stage of history as an adult, the first episode reported about him places him directly in the charismatic stream of Judaism. His mission began with a vision from the other world and the descent of the

Spirit upon him. At about the age of thirty, early in the governorship of Pontius Pilate,[6] something impelled Jesus to go to a wilderness preacher of repentance named John and known ever since as "John the Baptist." All of the Gospels (as well as Acts) connect the beginning of Jesus's ministry to his baptism by John.

Known to us from both the New Testament and the Jewish historian Josephus,[7] John stood in the charismatic stream of Judaism. His style of dress emulated Elijah's, and his contemporaries compared him to a prophet.[8] Renowned for his eloquent and passionate call for repentance, John proclaimed that it was not sufficient to be "children of Abraham"; the Jewish people were called to a more intense relationship to God sealed by a ritual of initiation (Mark 1:4–6; Matt. 3:7–10; Luke 3:7–9).[9] Crowds flocked to this charismatic, some to be baptized.

Jesus was among them. As he was being baptized by John, he had a vision.[10] It is very tersely described: "And just as he was coming up out of the water, he saw *the heavens torn apart and the Spirit descending like a dove on him*" (Mark 1:10).[11] The language recalls earlier experiences of the other world in the Jewish tradition. Like Ezekiel some six centuries before (1:1), Jesus saw "the heavens torn apart," momentarily seeing into the other world as if through a door or "tear." Through this door he saw "the Spirit descending . . . on him," echoing the words of an earlier Spirit-filled one: "The Spirit of the LORD God is upon me" (Isa. 61:1).[12]

The vision was accompanied by a "heavenly voice" that declared Jesus's identity to him: "You are my Son, the Beloved; with you I am well pleased" (Mark 1:11). About the historicity of the baptism and the vision itself, there is little reason for doubt. Unless we think that visions simply do not happen, there is no reason to deny this experience to Jesus. However, about the "heavenly voice" there is some historical uncertainty, simply because the words so perfectly express the post-Easter perception of Jesus's identity. As such, they must be historically suspect as the product of the followers of Jesus in the years after Easter.

Yet how we interpret the words affects the historical judgment. If "my Son, the Beloved" is taken to mean "unique" Son of God in the sense in which the church uses that term, then the phrase must be viewed as historically suspect. But if it is given the meaning that similar expressions have in stories of other Jewish charismatic holy men, then it is historically possible to imagine this as part of the experience of Jesus. They too had experiences in which a "heavenly voice" declared them to be God's "son."[3] If read in this way, the words not only become historically credible, but are a further link to charismatic Judaism.

Whatever the historical judgment concerning the "heavenly voice," the story of Jesus's vision places him in the Spirit-filled heart of Judaism. It reflects the multi-layered understanding of reality that was part of the belief system and actual experience of his predecessors in his own tradition. Indeed, standing as it does at the beginning of his ministry, the vision is reminiscent of the "call narratives" of the prophets. Like theirs, his ministry began with an intense experience of the Spirit of God.

The Course of Jesus's Ministry: A Person of Spirit

Jesus's ministry not only began with an experience of the Spirit, but was dominated throughout by intercourse with the other world.

Visions

The vision of the descent of the Spirit was followed immediately by another visionary experience or sequence of experiences. According to both Mark and the tradition behind Matthew and Luke, the Spirit "drove" or "led" Jesus out into the wilderness. Mark's account is very brief: "He was in the wilderness forty days, tempted by Satan; and he was with the wild beasts; and the angels waited on him" (1:13).

Matthew and Luke agree that he spent a forty-day solitude in the wilderness, where he was tested by the lord of the evil spirits and nourished by beneficent spirits. They add that Jesus fasted and had a series of three closely related visions (Matt. 4:1–11; Luke 4:1–13). In the first, Jesus was tempted by Satan to use his powers to change stones into bread. In the second and third, Jesus and Satan traveled together in the spirit world. The devil took Jesus to the highest point of the Temple in Jerusalem and then "showed him in an instant all the kingdoms of the world" (Luke 4:5; Matt. 4:8).[14] Throughout, Satan tempted Jesus to use his charismatic powers in self-serving ways and to give his allegiance to him in exchange for all the kingdoms of the world.

Both the setting and the content of the visions are noteworthy. Like Moses and Elijah and other Jewish holy men, Jesus journeyed into the wilderness, alone, beyond the domestication of reality provided by culture and human interchange. There, in a desolate desert area near the Dead Sea, he underwent a period of extended solitude and fasting, practices that produce changes in consciousness and perception and are typical of what other traditions call a "vision quest." Indeed, the *sequence* of initiation into the world of Spirit (the baptism) followed by a testing or ordeal in the wilderness is strikingly similar to what is reported of charismatic figures cross-culturally.[15]

The synoptic Gospels report one more visionary experience of Jesus. According to Luke, in the middle of his ministry, a group of Jesus's followers exclaimed: "Lord, in your name even the demons submit to us!" Jesus responded, "I watched Satan fall from heaven like a flash of lightning" (10:17–18). The passage uses language typically used to introduce a vision ("*I watched*"), though the passage could also be a metaphorical exclamation about the defeat of Satan.

We do not know if Jesus had other visions. The fact that none are reported may be without significance. Presumably,

Jesus would not routinely report such visions, but would do so only if they served some purpose in his teaching.[16] The rest of the New Testament frequently reports visions, suggesting that the early church continued to experience reality in the same Spirit-filled way that Jesus did.[17]

Prayer

Among the reasons that we in the modern world have difficulty giving credence to the reality of Spirit is the disappearance of the deeper forms of prayer from our experience. Most of us are aware primarily of a form of prayer in which God is addressed with words, whether out loud in the context of public prayer or internally in private prayer. Such "verbal prayer" is typically relatively brief, ordinarily no longer than a few minutes, perhaps sometimes longer in private devotion.

But verbal prayer is only one form of prayer in the Jewish-Christian tradition. Indeed, it is only the first stage of prayer; beyond it are deeper levels of prayer characterized by internal silence and lengthy periods of time. In this state, one enters into deeper levels of consciousness; ordinary consciousness is stilled, and one sits quietly in the presence of God. Typically called contemplation or meditation, its deepest levels are described as a communion or union with God.[18] One enters the realm of Spirit and experiences God.

For a variety of reasons, this form of prayer has become quite unfamiliar within the modern church. Though preserved in religious orders, by a few groups, and by individuals scattered throughout Christian denominations, it has largely disappeared as part of the experience of most people in modern culture.

The tradition in which Jesus stood knew this mode of prayer. Moses and Elijah spent long periods of time in solitude and communion with God. Nearer the time of Jesus, Galilean holy men regularly spent an hour "stilling their minds" in order to direct their hearts toward heaven.[19] Meditation also is found in Jewish mysticism. Though most familiar to us from the medieval Kabbalah, Jewish mysticism stretches back to the *merkabah* ("throne") mysticism of Jesus's time and before.[20] For the *merkabah* mystics, contemplative prayer was the vehicle for ascending through the heavens to the ultimate vision of beholding the throne of God—that is, of experiencing the kingship of God.

The Gospels portray Jesus as a man of prayer who practiced this form of prayer increasingly unknown in modern Western culture.[21] Like Moses and Elijah, he regularly withdrew into solitude for long hours of prayer: "In the morning, while it was still very dark, he got up and went out to a deserted place, and there he prayed" (Mark 1:35). Another time, "after saying farewell to them, he went up on the mountain to pray" (6:46). Luke reports that Jesus on occasion prayed all night (6:12).[22] Such lengthy hours of prayer accompanied by solitude do not imply verbal prayer, but contemplation or meditation, the stilling of the mind and directing of the heart toward God reported of Hanina ben Dosa and others in the Jewish spiritual tradition. Jesus practiced one of the classic disciplines for becoming present to the world of Spirit.

The intimacy of Jesus's experience of Spirit is pointed to by one of the distinctive features of his prayer life: his use of the word *Abba* to address God (Mark 14:36).[23] An Aramaic word used by very young children to address their father, *Abba* is like the English "Papa." Within Judaism, it was common to refer to God with the more formal "Father," but rare to call God *Abba*. The most plausible explanation for Jesus's departure from conventional usage is the intensity of his spiritual experience, a supposition supported by the parallel within Judaism. Namely, *Abba* is used as a term for God in traditions reported about Jewish charismatics contemporary with Jesus.[24] Thus at the heart of Jesus's prayer life was the experience of communion with God.

"The Spirit of the Lord Is upon Me"

The image of Jesus as a Spirit-filled person in the charismatic stream of Judaism is perfectly crystalized in the words with which, according to Luke, Jesus began his public ministry:

> The Spirit of the Lord is upon me, because
> he has anointed me to bring good news to the
> poor. He has sent me to proclaim release to the
> captives and recovery of sight to the blind, to let

the oppressed go free, to proclaim the year of the
Lord's favor. (4:18–19, quoting Isa. 61:1–2; 58:6)

About these words, quoted from an earlier charismatic
(Isaiah), Jesus then said, "Today this scripture has been
fulfilled in your hearing" (4:21). Though the passage as a
whole is often attributed to Luke and not to Jesus himself,[25] the picture of Jesus as one "anointed by the Spirit"
succinctly summarizes what we find in the Gospels. From
his baptism onward, through his ordeal in the wilderness
and continuing throughout his ministry, his life and mission were marked by an intense experiential relationship
to the Spirit.

Thus far we have been speaking about Jesus's *internal*
life: his prayer life, the visions he experienced, his sense
of intimacy with God. We also see his connection to the
world of Spirit in central dimensions of his public life: in
the impression he made on others, his claims to authority,
and the style of his speech.

The Impression Jesus Made on Others

In his classic book about the experience of the holy, or
the *numinous,* Rudolf Otto describes the *numinous presence* that frequently is felt in charismatic figures by those
around them. There is something uncanny about such
figures that evokes awe and amazement and impresses
people with the feeling of another world. There may be

something authoritative about the way they speak, penetrating about the way they see, powerful about their presence.[26]

Such was true of Jesus. A verse in Mark vividly conveys the impression he made, the "cloud of the *numinous*" that was present around him: "They were on the road, going up to Jerusalem, and Jesus was walking ahead of them; they were amazed, and those who followed were filled with awe" (10:32).[27]

As a teacher Jesus made a striking impression, very different from the official teachers: "They were astounded at his teaching, for he taught them as one having *authority,* and not as the scribes" (Mark 1:22). Behind the Greek word for "authority" lies the rabbinic term for the power or might of God, the *Gevurah:* "He speaks from the mouth of the *Gevurah,*"[28] that is, from the mouth of power or Spirit.

Popular opinion associated him with earlier charismatic figures, with Elijah, other prophets, or John the Baptist (Mark 6:14–16; 8:28; Matt. 21:11; Luke 7:12). The aura of "otherness" around him may explain the reaction of his family on one occasion: "They went out to restrain him, for people were saying, 'He has gone out of his mind'" (Mark 3:21).[29] Even his opponents granted that there was a spiritual power at work in him, but interpreted it as coming from "Beelzebul, the ruler of the demons" (3:22).

Not surprisingly, he attracted crowds: "The whole city was gathered around the door" (Mark 1:33); the paralytic could not be brought to him "because of the crowd" (2:4); and "a large crowd followed him and pressed in on him"

(5:24). Such language is only what we would expect in the early church's account of his ministry, but it also undoubtedly conveys the historical impression he made. Jesus was widely known as a charismatic figure, and it was this reputation as a man of Spirit that drew the crowds that flocked around him.

Jesus's Own Sense of Authority

Jesus himself was aware of this power or authority that others sensed in him. When some of the religious leaders in Jerusalem questioned him about his authority, Jesus responded with another question: "I will ask you one question; answer me, and I will tell you by what authority I do these things. Did the baptism of John come from heaven, or was it of human origin?" (Mark 11:29–30).[30] Was the authority of John "from heaven," from the "other world," or from humans? Though unexpressed, Jesus's own view is clear: implicitly he claimed the same authority as John, one grounded neither in institution nor tradition but in the Spirit.

Similarly, Jesus was aware of the power of the Spirit flowing through him. In the context of casting out a demon, he identified the power as the Spirit of God: "If it is by *the Spirit of God* that I cast out demons, then the kingdom of God has come to you" (Matt. 12:28).[31] On another occasion, after a woman had touched his garment in order to be healed, he perceived that *power* had gone forth from him (Mark 5:30).

The style of Jesus's teaching also shows an awareness of a *numinous* authority not derived from tradition. It is seen in his emphatic and unusual "I say to you" (or "I tell you") statements, often prefaced in an unprecedented manner with "Amen" ("Truly," "Certainly"; e.g., "Truly I tell you . . ."), a solemn formula that normally followed a statement.[32] Sometimes his emphatic "I say to you" was incorporated into a contrast with the words of the tradition using the pattern, "You have heard that it was said . . . but I say to you . . ."[33] Thus the language of Jesus indicates an awareness of a tradition-transcending authority, one from the mouth of the Spirit.

Moreover, he called disciples, an action that points to his sense of charismatic authority even as it also testifies to the deep impression he made on people. Though it was relatively common for a teacher within Judaism to have devoted students, the phenomenon of discipleship is different and uncommon, involving an uprooting and a following after. The stories of the call of the disciples describe with compact vividness the imperative of Jesus's call, the immediacy of their response, and the radical rupture from their previous lives:

> As Jesus passed along the Sea of Galilee, he saw Simon and his brother Andrew casting a net in the sea—for they were fishermen. And Jesus said to them, "Follow me and I will make you fish for people." And immediately they left their nets and followed him. As he went a little farther, he saw

James son of Zebedee and his brother John, who
were in their boat mending the nets. Immediately
he called them; and they left their father Zebedee
in the boat with the hired men, and followed
him. (Mark 1:16–20)[34]

Later, one of them exclaimed: "Look, we have *left everything* and followed you" (Mark 10:28). The phenomenon
of discipleship is located within the charismatic stream of
Judaism, occurring in response to a charismatic leader.[35]

Given all of the above, it is not surprising that Jesus
had a prophetic consciousness. Not only did some of his
contemporaries put him in the prophetic tradition, but he
also twice referred to himself as a prophet, albeit somewhat indirectly. In his hometown, he said, "Prophets are
not without honor, except in their hometown, and among
their own kin, and in their own house" (Mark 6:4). Later
he said, "It is impossible for a prophet to be killed outside
of Jerusalem" (Luke 13:33). Identifying himself with the
prophets, Jesus saw himself in the tradition of those who
knew God.[36]

The Transfiguration

Some of the disciples reportedly experienced a strange episode that underlines the connection between Jesus and the
world of Spirit. According to Mark, shortly before Jesus
began his final journey to Jerusalem, the inner core of the
disciples momentarily saw him transformed, his form and

clothing suffused with light. Jesus "led them up a high mountain apart, by themselves. And he was transfigured before them, and his clothes became dazzling white. . . . And there appeared to them Elijah with Moses, who were talking to Jesus" (Mark 9:2–4).[37]

The details link Jesus to the world of the charismatics. Like Moses before him, he momentarily "glowed" with the radiance of the Spirit (stories of "glowing" holy men are also reported elsewhere). With him were seen Elijah and Moses, the two great charismatic figures of the Jewish tradition.[38] Of course, it is very difficult to know what to make of the story historically. Did the disciples actually have this experience, or is the whole narrative a symbolic statement of Jesus's identity? But even if the narrative is viewed as the creation of the church, it remains significant that the tradition associated Jesus with the two great men of Spirit of Israel's history.

Jesus's Own Sense of Identity

Jesus himself, his contemporaries, and the Gospel writers all identified him with the charismatic stream of Judaism, as having a consciousness akin to that of the prophets. Did he also think of himself with the exalted titles with which the early church proclaimed him after Easter? Did he think of himself as the Messiah (Christ)? Or as the "Son of God"? As already noted, historical scholarship has tended to give a negative answer.[39] But, as with the "heavenly voice" at his baptism, the historical judgment hinges in part upon the sense in which these terms are understood.

If "Son of God" is used in the special Christian sense that emerges in the rest of the New Testament (by the time of Paul and John, preexistent with God from before creation; by the time of Matthew and Luke, conceived by the Spirit and born of a virgin), then almost certainly Jesus did not think of himself as *the* Son of God. But if "son of God" is given the meaning that it carried within Judaism at the time of Jesus, then it is possible he did. There, "son of God" was used in three different contexts to refer to three different entities, though with a common nuance of meaning. In the Hebrew Bible, it referred to Israel as a whole or to the king of Israel.[40] Contemporary with Jesus, the image of God as father and a particular person as God's son was used, as already noted, in stories about Jewish charismatic holy men. All three uses have one element in common. All designate a relationship of special intimacy with God— Israel as the chosen people, the king as the adopted son, the charismatic as one who knows and is known by God.

In this Jewish sense, Jesus may have thought of himself as "son of God." He clearly was aware of a relationship of special intimacy. His use of the term *Abba* has as its corollary the term "son." In a number of passages that may plausibly be attributed to him he uses father-and-son imagery to speak at least indirectly of his relationship to God. Finally, the use of the image by other Jewish charismatics contemporary with him, with whom he shared much in common, provides a context in which the term is not only appropriate but virtually expected.

Moreover, there is a web of associations connecting this experiential awareness of intimacy with God with the term "Messiah." "Messiah" (*mashiah*) in the Jewish scriptures means simply "anointed," that is, "smeared with oil." Such anointing was part of the coronation of the king of Israel, who thereby became God's "son." Jesus was aware of both "sonship" and being anointed by the Spirit, as we have seen. Thus the phrases "anointed by God" and "son of God" and the term "Messiah" are all closely related.

We cannot know if Jesus made these associations himself; no saying that does this explicitly can be confidently attributed to him. Moreover, we may surmise that he did not spend a great deal of time thinking about who he was. Finally, of course, it does not matter whether he thought of himself as Messiah or Son of God, for his identity as either of those does not depend on whether he thought so.[41] Yet our exploration of his life as a Spirit-filled person shows that the church's exalted designations of him were not arbitrary impositions, but had roots in the historical experience of Jesus himself.

Jesus's intense relationship to the world of Spirit thus enables us not only to glimpse what he was like as a historical figure, but also to understand the origin and appropriateness of the titles with which he was later proclaimed. Clearly, Easter played the major role in leading the followers of Jesus to describe him in the most glorious terms known in his culture. Yet the seeds of the church's proclamation lie in the experience of the historical Jesus, even if the full-grown plant needed the experience of Easter to allow it to burst forth.

The cumulative impression created by the synoptic Gospels is very strong: Jesus stood in the charismatic tradition of Judaism, which reached back to the beginnings of Israel. Matthew, Mark, and Luke all portray him as a Spirit-filled person through whom the power of Spirit flowed. His relationship to Spirit was both the source of and the energy for the mission he undertook. According to these earliest portraits, Jesus was one who knew the other world, who stood in a long line of mediators stretching back to Elijah and Moses. Indeed, according to them, he was the climax of that history of mediation. Moreover, Jesus's relationship to the world of Spirit is also the key for understanding the central dimensions of his ministry: as healer, sage, revitalization movement founder, and prophet.

Chapter 5

Reclaiming Mysticism

Jesus as Spirit Person and Prophet

A Spirit person is one known for his or her intimacy with
the sacred and for the ability to perform miracles. Here I
wish to comment further about the first dimension of a
Spirit person's experience. Namely, a Spirit person is not
only a channel for primordial power, but *knows* that power.
Essential to a Spirit person's experience is the "breaking of
plane," frequently expressed as movement in a vertical
direction. This involves both alteration of consciousness
and movement in a new dimension, often symbolized
by a "celestial pole" that permits mystical ascent to the

Originally published in *Conflict, Holiness, and Politics in the Teachings
of Jesus* (1984).

heavens.[1] As such, a Spirit person's experience is one form of mystical experience, a union or communion with God, or even with "God beyond God," that is, with Reality itself, that which lies behind all conceptualizations, including all conceptions of God. Those who have such experiences speak of them as ineffable, incapable of being described precisely, for the experience is beyond thought and beyond the subject-object distinction or classification that both thought and language presuppose.

Yet those who have such experiences also insist that it is a *knowing,* and not just a feeling; it is a noetic and not simply a subjective emotional state. The knowing is direct, immediate, intuitive, quite unlike the modern Western understanding of knowledge as necessarily involving observer and observed and thus subject-object separation.[2] Some mystics describe the experience as one of union in which self and God merge indistinguishably, others as a communion in which self and God interpenetrate but "particularity" somehow remains, a difference generally (though not universally) characteristic of Eastern and Western mysticism respectively.[3]

This way of knowing God was present in Jesus's milieu. There were other Jewish Spirit persons contemporary with Jesus.[4] Moreover, Jewish mysticism is known to antedate the time of Jesus. Though all of its extant literary products come from a later period beginning with the oldest Hekhaloth books from no later than the third century CE in Palestine,[5] Jewish mysticism clearly had its roots much earlier, at least as early as the first century BCE.[6] Furthermore, quite apart from tracing a literary tradition, it is clear that this way of knowing God is very ancient in the Jewish tradition. Moses and Elijah were the two Spirit persons par excellence in the Hebrew Bible, and the prophets of ancient Israel knew God in this intimate way.[7]

That Jesus knew God in this manner is apparent not only from his sharing the general characteristics of a Spirit person, but from specific indications in the synoptic texts. The intimacy of his knowing is reflected in his addressing God in prayer as *Abba* (Mark 14:36), an informal Aramaic word used by very young children for their father that may perhaps be translated "Papa," which points to the intimate experience of the divine. The usage is very uncommon in Judaism, where the few parallels are found in rabbinic texts about other Jewish Spirit persons.[8] Closely related to this point, a Q text[9] reports that Jesus spoke of the intimate knowing that occurs between father and son and used this analogy to speak of his own experience of God: "No one knows the Son except the Father, and no one knows the Father except the Son" (Matt. 11:27; Luke 10:22).[10] The two halves of the statement are a Semitic idiom that means simply, "Only father and son really know each other," the Semitic way of speaking of a reciprocal relationship of knowing and being known by.[11]

Thus, as a Jewish Spirit person, Jesus knew God. Out of this intimate knowing flowed his understanding of God's nature or quality and his perception of what Israel was to be. Among the passages that give expression to Jesus's understanding of God's nature is the classic Q text:

> Look at the birds of the air; they neither sow nor reap nor gather into barns, and yet your heavenly Father feeds them. Are you not of more value than they? And can any of you by worrying add a single hour to your span of life? And why do you worry about clothing? Consider the lilies of the field, how they grow; they neither toil nor spin, yet I tell you, even Solomon in all his glory was not clothed like one of these. But if God so clothes the grass of the field, which is alive today and tomorrow is thrown into the oven, will he not much more clothe you—you of little faith? (Matt. 6:26–30; Luke 12:24–28)

According to another Q text, Jesus said:

> Are not five sparrows sold for two pennies? Yet not one of them is forgotten in God's sight. But even the hairs of your head are all counted. Do not be afraid; you are of more value than many sparrows. (Luke 12:6–7; Matt. 5:29–30)

In these texts, marked by an imaginative and poetic appeal to nature, Jesus invited his hearers to see reality as characterized by a cosmic generosity. God feeds the birds, clothes the grass with lily blossoms, knows every sparrow, numbers every hair. Even those things that have little value to human beings have value to God: the grass thrown into the oven, the sparrows sold in the marketplace five for two pennies. Reality is permeated, indeed flooded, with divine creativity, nourishment, and care.

To see God as gracious, nourishing, and encompassing is consistent with the Hebrew Bible and the tradition in which Jesus stood.[12] But the freshness of imagery and intensity of expression in these texts require more of an explanation than tradition. The most satisfactory explanation is that he knew God in his own experience.

The depiction of ultimate reality as lavishly nourishing care upon creation without regard to human valuation is intrinsically connected to the understanding of God as compassionate. The same cosmic munificence that clothes the grass also "makes the sun rise on the evil and the good, and sends rain on the righteous and on the unrighteous" (Matt. 5:45). This perception flowed from Jesus's own subjective experience of the *mysterium tremendum* as gracious and compassionate, encompassing and present. As a Spirit person who knew the nature of the sacred, the "numinous," from his own experience, Jesus proclaimed the acceptance of the outcasts in both his teaching and actions. Moreover, his articulation of inclusive compassion as the paradigm for Israel to follow was similarly grounded in his own experience. Thus Jesus's basic "program" for the internal reform of Israel—"Be compassionate as God is compassionate" (Luke 6:36)—flowed out of knowledge of God that he, as a Spirit person, was given in his own internal experience.

The sense of mission that he received as a Spirit person led him to undertake the role of prophet. As a prophet, he aggressively and provocatively challenged the corporate direction of his people. Violating the taboos of table fellowship, subverting the Sabbath, criticizing traditions regarding the Temple, he reversed the expectations of the future held by his contemporaries. Motivated by a profound love for his own people in a time when their future was at stake, he repudiated the burgeoning momentum leading toward armed resistance to Rome and called his hearers to the path of peace. His table fellowship, because it included quislings and publicly enacted the breakdown of holiness as separation, pointed to an understanding of Israel different from that advocated by those seeking a holy, separated nation.

He also repudiated the Temple ideology that augmented the dynamic of resistance with the expectation of success. Contingent upon Israel's response, Jesus promised peace instead of war, most evidently in Luke 19:42–44, in which he spoke not only of peace but, by contrasting the way of peace to the impending destruction of Jerusalem, made it clear that peace was not merely a depoliticized spiritual experience but embraced political peace. Peace as a consequence of response to Jesus was also implied in Jesus's acted fulfillment of Zechariah 9:9 in the entry into Jerusalem narrative.[13]

The admonition "love your enemy" would have been understood as an explicit reference to the Roman enemy and an unmistakable command to eschew the path of armed resistance. The saying, a source of perennial debate in Christian ethics, was in fact intended not simply for personal relationships, but as "public policy" at a particular time in history toward a particular state.[14] In an episode reported only by John but with allusive support in Mark (John 6:14–15; Mark 6:30–44), Jesus spurned the attempt of a desert gathering to make him king, that is, the leader of a national liberation movement, vetoing resistance as the way for Israel, though the incident also hints that Jesus was more concerned with national issues than is often affirmed.[15]

Finally, the most famous pronouncement in this connection, "Give therefore to the emperor the things that are the emperor's, and to God the things that are God's" (Mark 12:17), must be regarded as answering the question about the tribute tax, even though it was probably not as important as it is usually claimed to be.[16] The tax was to be paid, and as such it was a pronouncement that radicalized anti-Roman elements could not have endorsed.[17]

To this disavowal of national resistance, two qualifications must be added at once. First, it did not imply a positive evaluation of Roman imperial order, for the Roman emperor was undoubtedly to be numbered among those who lorded it over their subjects, which was an object lesson of how not to behave.[18] It was Rome that committed atrocities, that would destroy Jerusalem, that would commit the abomination of desolation, that thereby, indeed, was

Nebuchadnezzar *redivivus,* Antiochus *redivivus*. Rome was no more viewed as good than Assyria and Babylon were viewed as good by the preexilic prophets. Herod Antipas, the local incarnation of Gentile power, was described contemptuously as "that fox" (Luke 13:32).[19]

Second, because of this reversal of Israel's political aspirations, the injunction to nonresistance, and the advice to pay tribute, Jesus is widely held to be nonpolitical. But such a conclusion is incorrect. Jesus's attitude toward Rome was not based on an apolitical stance, but on the conviction that in the political affairs of the world the judging activity of God was at work. Regarding his own society, he was intensely political in the sense we have given to that term: he was concerned about the institutions and historical dynamic of Israel. The means he used, including public revolutionary gestures, challenged current practice. The end he sought was the transformation of the cultural dynamic of the quest for holiness into a cultural dynamic that would conform Israel to God as compassionate.

As a prophet, Jesus called Israel to a national reorientation in which both attitudes and institutions would be conformed to the inclusive compassion of God. Such a reorientation included a repudiation both of the path of resistance and of the quest for holiness that sustained it. This national reorientation is included in the word "repent," which, though it does not appear frequently in the teachings of Jesus, is joined to the programmatic summation of Jesus's preaching in Mark 1:15: "The kingdom of

God has come near; repent." For repentance, though done by individuals, was not a turning from individual sins so much as a turning from a certain understanding of God and Israel to a transformed understanding.[20] It called for a departure from the established structures that had shaped and nurtured the existence of those who heard Jesus to a new understanding of Israel as a community of inclusive compassion that would allow it to face a future that was largely unknown, with only the promise that ultimately God would vindicate them.

Repentance so understood entailed risks. There was not only a risk to the individual who responded, but also a risk to the existence of Israel, for the function of Torah and Temple *as institutions preservative of Israel's cohesiveness* would largely disappear if they were subordinated to the paradigm of compassion. Indeed, the perception of the importance of these institutions for Israel's survival was a fundamental reason for the opposition offered to Jesus by his contemporaries. What seemed threatened by the transformation of these institutions was national identity and national survival itself. Yet what was called for was a course of reckless abandon in a time when the destiny of Israel was at stake.

Thus, like the classical prophets of the Hebrew Bible, Jesus sought to divert his people from a course that was leading to catastrophe. Apparently knowing that the likely outcome would be his death, he went to Jerusalem during the season of Passover, there to make one final dramatic appeal to his people at the center of their corporate life.

Jesus as Sage: The Importance of the Heart

Jesus also appears in the role of sage, a teacher of wisdom. Sages are important figures in traditional cultures. Classic examples are Lao Tzu in sixth-century BCE China, the Buddha, and the authors of the wisdom tradition in the Hebrew Bible: Proverbs, Job, Ecclesiastes. Vast in its scope, ranging from matters that are virtually questions of etiquette to ultimate matters such as human nature and the nature of ultimate reality, the source of sagely teaching is reflection upon existence from a particular perspective. To put that negatively, its source is not revealed esoteric truths from another world or deductions logically derived from an authoritative tradition (even though the tradition may affect the sage's reflection). The authority of the teaching depends upon its own perspicacity rather than upon some external authority. Frequently sages use analogies drawn from nature or common human experience to illustrate what they are seeking to communicate, thus inviting their hearers to see things a certain way rather than insisting that tradition or revelation dictate a particular way of seeing things. The parables and aphoristic sayings of Jesus (and other figures in his tradition) are good examples of this.

The perspective from which the astute observations flow is commonly age, that is, from reflection upon experience over many years. Frequently an older person, the sage has observed much and pondered long, and many cultures associate wisdom with "the elders." Occasionally and remarkably, sagacity is found in younger persons, as in Jesus and the Buddha. In such instances, the vantage point is obviously not the product of age. Rather, the transformation of perception is the product of the sages' spiritual experience. The mystical perception of both self and world is *sub specie aeternitatis,* a vantage point beyond time from which ordinary consciousness and experience seem like a state of estrangement. Indeed, the stronger the mystical perspective, the more sharply ordinary existence appears to be a life of blindness, bondage, and misery, a plight that triggers compassion, sadness, and sometimes even anger. When this experience is combined with a sagacious intellect, the result is insight.

As a sage whose perception flowed out of his experience of the sacred, Jesus developed a set of teachings about God, the human predicament, and the way of transformation. In this section, we shall focus on his perception of the way of transformation.

Like the teaching of other renewal movements, Jesus's teaching also involved an intensification of the Torah.[21] The other renewal movements intensified the Torah in the direction of holiness, emphasizing various forms of separation—from society as a whole, from the Gentiles, from impurity within society. Jesus, however, intensified the Torah primarily by applying it to internal dimensions of the human psyche: to dispositions, emotions, thoughts, and desires. Moreover, as we shall see near the end of this section, this internalization had immediate socioreligious and politico-religious consequences.

Jesus's application of Torah to internal dispositions can be seen most clearly in the antitheses of the Sermon on the Mount. Some of these most likely go back to Jesus himself, and all of them provide evidence for the stance of the Jesus movement. Not just killing, but also anger is prohibited; not just adultery, but also lust is enjoined (Matt. 5:21–22, 27–28). Such is also the thrust of the saying in Mark 7:15: "There is nothing outside a person that by going in can defile, but the things that come out are what defile." That is, what matters is what is within; true purity is a matter of inward purity. In Mark, the passage continues:

> Do you not see that whatever goes into a person
> from outside cannot defile, since it enters, not
> the heart but the stomach and goes out into the
> sewer? . . . It is what comes out of a person that
> defiles. For it is from within, from the human
> heart, that evil intentions come: fornication, theft,
> murder, adultery, avarice, wickedness, deceit,
> licentiousness, envy, slander, pride, folly. All these
> evil things come from within, and they defile a
> person. (7:18–23)

Though almost certainly Marcan and not to be attributed to Jesus, the words are an appropriate commentary, extending the meaning of the previous saying and explicitly introducing the notion of the heart. Impurity is a matter of the heart, not of external behavior. Indeed, the latter has its source in the former. Conversely, true purity is purity of heart, as Jesus is reported to have said on another occasion: "Blessed are the pure in heart, for they shall see God" (Matt. 5:8).

The intensification of Torah by applying it to what is internal is thus seen most centrally in Jesus's teaching concerning the heart. In Jewish psychology, as disclosed in both the Hebrew Bible and the rabbinic tradition, the heart is "the psyche at its deepest level," "the innermost spring of individual life, the ultimate source of all its physical, intellectual, emotional, and volitional energies."[22] As such, the heart is the seat or source of thinking, feeling, and behavior, of intellect, emotion, and will. They do not shape or control the heart; it shapes them. The rabbinic tradition affirmed that the heart in turn was ruled either by the "evil inclination" (*ha-yetzer ha-ra*) or the "good inclination" (*ha-yetzer ha-tob*).[23] The power of the evil impulse was great: like a king, it ruled the 248 parts of the body. According to other images, the evil inclination ensnared the self with threads that, though thin as a spider's web at the beginning, soon became as thick as a ship's rope. Beginning as a visitor in the heart, it became a regular guest, and finally the host.[24] Thus one could have either a good or evil heart; the self at its deepest level could be inclined (or driven) either of two ways.

Jesus accepted this understanding of the heart and made it central to his perception of the human condition. In a passage attested by both Matthew and Luke, he said:

> No good tree bears bad fruit, nor again does a
> bad tree bear good fruit; for each tree is known

by its own fruit. For figs are not gathered from thorns, nor are grapes picked from a bramble bush. The good person out of the good treasure of the heart produces good, and the evil person out of evil treasure produces evil; for it is out of the abundance of the heart that the mouth speaks. (Luke 6:43–45; Matt. 12:33–35; cf. Matt. 7:16–20)

As a sage, Jesus made a commonsense observation about nature: one gathers figs and grapes from fig trees and vines, not from thorn or bramble bushes. The application of the observation is obvious and far-reaching: the tree and its fruits are an image for the self (the heart) and its behavior: a good self produces good behavior. The rest of the saying makes explicit the connection to the heart: a heart filled with good treasure produces good, and one filled with evil treasure produces evil. Thus what matters is the kind of tree one is, the kind of heart one has.

Just as the rabbis spoke of the heart being inclined one of two different ways, so did Jesus. Identifying two comprehensive centers of ultimate loyalty, Jesus spoke of "treasures in heaven" and "treasures on earth," symbolic of the infinite and finite respectively, and added, "Where your treasure is, there will your heart be also" (Matt. 6:19–21; cf. Luke 12:33–34). That is, if one's treasure is in the finite, "where moth and rust consume and where thieves break in and steal," then one's heart will be preoccupied with the finite.

The same two fundamental orientations appear in a passage in which Jesus spoke of the impossibility of serving two masters: "You cannot serve God and wealth" (Matt. 6:24; Luke 16:13). "Wealth" by extension connoted all of the finite. The heart could be centered in God or the finite, the servant (slave) of one or the other. Thus what made a heart pure or impure was its center.

Apparently, Jesus perceived most of his contemporaries as centered in the finite. In his parables, whose power depends upon the realistic portrayal of typical human behavior, people are concerned to receive what is theirs, undisposed to be generous to others, anxious about losing what they have, and fearful of defilement. In his teaching, he regularly identified four centers as most typically dominant in people's lives: family, status, possessions, and piety. The last perception is particularly interesting. The heart can center in its own piety, its own holiness or purity, whether one ostentatiously displays it or not, for the fault lies not in displaying the piety but in holding to it as the basis of identity and distinction from others. Such a heart is not pure, as the conclusion of the parable of the Pharisee and the tax collector (Luke 18:9–14) shows: the tax collector, who appealed to the mercy of God and prayed for a pure heart, was praised instead of the Pharisee, who centered on his own purity.

Thus the problem was the heart: what mattered was a pure heart. Centuries earlier, the author of Psalm 51 identified the problem in the same manner: "Create in me a clean heart, O God, and put a new and right spirit within me" (51:10). The hope for a transformed heart was the basis of the new covenant of which Jeremiah spoke:

> But this is the covenant that I will make with the house of Israel after those days says the LORD: I will put my law within them, and I will write it *on their hearts;* and I will be their God, and they shall be my people. No longer shall they teach one another, or say to each other, "Know the LORD," for they shall all know me, from the least of them to the greatest. (31:33–34)

Significantly, the passage combines the internalization of the Torah "upon their hearts" with *knowing* God.

What was needed was a new heart. But how was the heart to be transformed? Obedience to the Torah was one way; indeed, the purpose of the Torah was to "incline one's heart toward God." Immersion in and meticulous observance of Torah in virtually every aspect of daily life reminded one constantly of God and, with the Torah more and more internalized within the psyche, oriented the heart toward God. Moreover, it worked. Judaism produced a number of notable saints through this method.

However, this way had become normative among the religious, in part because of the particular circumstances facing Judaism in the Roman period and because of the particular intensifications of Torah that had established holiness as the exclusive way of being rightly related to God and as a blueprint for society. But as the normative way, this way cut off large numbers—perhaps most—of the Jewish people from a relationship to God and was responsible for the division within the people of God between the righteous and the outcast. Moreover, in Jesus's perception, it was possible to posture this way, to follow the requirements of holiness without being transformed: "Isaiah prophesied rightly about you hypocrites, as it is written, 'This people honors me with their lips, but their heart is far from me'" (Mark 7:6).

Jesus spoke of another way of transformation. Most basically, it was the path of death: "If any want to become my followers, let them deny themselves and take up their cross and follow me" (Mark 8:34).[25] In the first century, crucifixion was widely known in Palestine as a form of execution practiced by the Romans—a slow, torturous, agonizing death inflicted upon those suspected of treason against the power that ruled the world. Customarily the condemned were required to carry the horizontal crossbeam to the place of execution; hence, "bearing one's cross" was a stark symbol for death. The language of "following," "coming after," points to the image of a way or path. To follow after Jesus, to follow his way, meant walking the road to death—to deny one's self and take up the cross.

Even though some of the early followers of Jesus were literally crucified, the saying was metaphorical, as the earliest commentary on it suggests: "Let them deny themselves and take up their cross *daily*" (Luke 9:23).[26] As a metaphor for an internal spiritual process, the "path of death" involved the death of the heart centered in the finite and the birth of a new heart centered in God. The way of death can be described either as a dying to the world or a dying to the self: the person dies to the world as the center of security and to the self as the center of concern. From this death emerges a new or pure heart centered in God.

Many of the images and contrasts in the teaching of Jesus expressed this basic pattern. To become as a servant was to cease to have a will of one's own, for servants/slaves in the ancient world were understood to be agents of their master's will. Their will had died (Mark 9:33–35; Mark 10:42–44; Matt. 20:25–27; cf. Luke 22:25–26; Matt. 23:11). To become as a child was to become as an infant, a newborn (Matt. 18:2–4; Mark 10:15; Luke 18:17).[27]

In words preserved four times in the Gospel tradition, Jesus contrasted humbling and exaltation: "All who exalt themselves will be humbled, but all who humble themselves will be exalted" (Luke 18:14; see also Luke 14:11; Matt. 23:12; 18:4). Self-exaltation or self-elevation is a natural response of the self to culturally validated accomplishment, for the culture's standards have been internalized within the self through the process of socialization, and the self that meets those standards thus judges itself "good." In the Gospel contexts of this saying, these standards are religious and social.[28] The self in its own eyes thus "stands out" and becomes the basis for self-affirmation; it and its status have become the center.

"Self-humbling" is the opposite. In the Hebrew Bible, to be humble was often associated with the objective state of poverty and affliction,[29] but by the first century referred

primarily to a subjective state, though still carrying connotations of poverty. To be humble was not to claim status, but to be internally without possessions, to be empty.[30]
Self-humbling was thus self-emptying, and the passage
may be paraphrased, "Those who empty themselves will
be exalted; those who exalt themselves will be emptied,
will come to naught."

The closely parallel contrasts of *first* and *last, finding one's
life* and *losing one's life* made basically the same point. Those
who make themselves first will be last, and those who put
themselves last shall be first (Mark 10:31; Luke 13:30;
Matt. 20:16); those who seek their lives will lose them, but
those who let go of their lives will find them (Matt. 10:39; cf.
Mark 8:35 and parallels; Luke 17:33; cf. John 12:25).

The way as the path of death and rebirth of a new heart
was embodied in the life and teaching of the early Christian movement. The apostle Paul, the earliest of the New
Testament authors, wrote, "I have been crucified with
Christ; and it is no longer I who live, but it is Christ who
lives in me" (Gal. 2:19–20), and he affirmed that this experience was common to all Christians.[31] Such was also
the case in the Jesus movement in Palestine, which grew
directly out of Jesus's teaching. The symbolism of baptism,
its ritual of initiation, points intrinsically to death and resurrection, to new creation: one was plunged beneath the
waters of death and returned to the night before creation,
where one was created anew, born anew.

The Jesus movement in Palestine not only preserved the
teaching of Jesus concerning the path of death, but arranged

it into comprehensive patterns that emphasized the teaching even more sharply. Mark's Gospel as a whole can be construed as the Gospel of "the way"[32] and the massive central section of Luke's Gospel (9:51–18:14) as a journey toward death.[33]

The way of transformation of which Jesus spoke was akin to his own experience. Intrinsic to the spirituality of a Spirit person is the internal experience of the death of self, sometimes involving a ritual of self-wounding, an ordeal, or participation in a myth of dismemberment that corresponds to inner psychic experience.[34] Jesus's ministry began with a ritual of death and rebirth, baptism; strikingly, the Gospels agree that on this occasion Jesus's identity as "son" was first disclosed. Moreover, the baptism was followed immediately by the temptation in the wilderness, which can be understood as a Spirit person's initiatory ordeal and encounter with the Spirit world. Jesus himself had "died to the world," living without possessions, family, or home. Yet he did not make the details of his way normative, but only the basic pattern itself.

Put positively, the path of death involved trusting radically in the compassion of God and letting go of the self and the world as the basis of security and focus of concern. This way was simultaneously hard and easy. It was hard especially for those who were quite secure and who measured up to the standards of culture internalized within their psyches, whether the decisive standards were wealth, status, or observance of the Torah.

For them to let go of those standards and the self that met them was very difficult. Hence the way was the *narrow* way: "The gate is narrow and the road is hard that leads to life, and there are few who find it" (Matt. 7:14; cf. Luke 13:24).

Hence also the metaphor of death: dying is very hard and it is difficult to let go of finite centers. Yet it was also the easy way because it was a "letting go," a cessation of striving. Moreover, it may have been easier for some, namely, the poor and the outcasts. Riches were not a temptation for the poor (except in societies that stress upward mobility); the poor knew that the world offered a scant measure of security. Righteousness was not a temptation for the sinner, social approval not a snare for the outcast. To die to a world in which one was poor, that pronounced one an outcast, was not as difficult as dying to a world in which one was financially secure, socially and religiously esteemed. Hence Jesus could say:

> Come to me, all you that are weary and are
> carrying heavy burdens, and I will give you rest.
> Take my yoke upon you, and learn from me; for
> I am gentle and humble in heart, and you will
> find rest for your souls. For my yoke is easy, and
> my burden is light. (Matt. 11:28–30)

The way of transformation thus involved becoming pure in heart through dying to the finite and living by radical trust in God. The world as the center of existence comes to an end. The form as well as the content of much of the sagely teaching of Jesus seemed designed to jolt his hearers out of their present world, their present way of seeing reality. The aphoristic sayings and parables are crystallized flashes of insight that also compel insight and frequently reverse ordinary understanding by bringing it into judgment. In short, even the form of Jesus's wisdom teaching mediated and invited end-of-world.[35]

Thus Jesus proclaimed a way of transformation that did not depend upon observing the requirements of the Torah as understood by the other renewal movements. Speaking of a divine compassion grounded in his own experience of God, he proclaimed a way of transformation whereby people could increasingly experience and live that awareness. By undergoing that path, they began the process of becoming good trees producing good fruit, of having hearts whose treasure was in heaven. Thus Jesus internalized holiness, just as he internalized the commandments against murder and adultery. Holiness was a matter of the heart, for what mattered was a pure heart. The way to purity of heart was not exclusively or even primarily through obedience to the Torah, but the path of dying to the self and the world.

Those commentators throughout the centuries who have affirmed that Jesus was centrally concerned with the orientation and transformation of the heart are thus correct. What has not often been noted, however, is that Jesus's teaching about the heart had a number of immediate socioreligious and historical-political implications in the context of the Jewish homeland in the first century. Affirming that purity was a matter of the heart cut the connection between holiness and separation as understood by the other renewal movements. That is, holiness was to be achieved neither by driving the Romans from the land nor by withdrawal from society nor by separation within society. Intensifying the Torah by applying it to purity of heart also destroyed the basis for dividing society into the righteous and the outcast, for "once the norms had been intensified . . . so that they were quite beyond the possibility of fulfillment," applying to internal disposition as well as behavior, no group could claim that it alone was the "true Israel," for "all alike were sinners."[36] Jesus's teaching thereby provided a ground for overcoming the fragmentation of Jewish society.[37]

Moreover, Jesus perceived that the orientation of the heart—its most deeply seated commitments—had historical-political consequences. He saw that the most fundamental commitments of his culture were leading to a collision course with Rome. Finally, the basic quality of a heart centered in God—compassion—had political implications. Compassion was to be the core value of the people of God as a historical community. Thus Jesus's teaching as sage was not divorced from the conflict situation for which we have argued, but was integral to it.

Chapter 6

Awe, Wonder, and Jesus

PERHAPS NO ASPECT of the Gospel portrait of Jesus poses so many difficulties for the modern mind as the tradition that he was a "wonder-worker," a performer of "miracles." As a culture, we do not take it for granted that there are "miraculous powers" at work in the world, and we are suspicious of events that seem to require an explanation that transcends what we take to be the "natural" laws of cause and effect. Except in cases where a psychosomatic explanation seems possible, miracles violate the modern sense of what is possible.

Originally published in *Jesus: A New Vision* (1987).

Within the church itself there is uncertainty about the miraculous elements in the Gospels. Christians in mainstream churches, those most open to the intellectual spirit and genuine achievements of the modern age, share in our culture's suspicion and tend to ignore the miracle stories of Jesus or else interpret them in such a way that no violation of the modern understanding of what is possible occurs. More "conservative" and fundamentalist Christians tend to insist that the miracles *really* happened and suspect that those who are uncertain about their historical actuality do not really believe in the power of God. Some even argue that the miracles "prove" that Jesus was divine, turning them into an element in a tight rational argument. For charismatic Christians, the emphasis is different. Rather than seeing the miracles as unique and thus as "proofs" of who Jesus was, they are convinced that the same "gifts of the Spirit" are still accessible and operative today. Understandably, they find no difficulty believing that such powers flowed through Jesus.

Modern biblical scholarship has developed its own characteristic approach.[1] Concerned with the meaning of the miracle stories as part of the *early church's story of Jesus,* it has not been very much concerned with the historicity (the actual "happenedness") of the miracles. The concern has been with what the Gospel writers intended to say with the miracle stories as components of a larger narrative or literary unit, the Gospels themselves. Such meanings are disclosed by paying meticulous attention to the relationship of a particular miracle story to the Gospel in which it is found, including its use of recurrent themes or motifs that are important to the author and to its placement within a particular Gospel. Attention is also paid to the relationship between the miracle stories and the larger literary-religious tradition of which they are a part. The early Christians who put the miracle stories of Jesus into their present form did so not only in light of their post-Easter experience of the living Christ, but also as part of a rich literary-religious tradition constituted by the Jewish religion and the Hebrew Bible (which was still their sacred scripture). Not surprisingly, they often alluded to their tradition as they told their stories about Jesus.

For example, the story of Jesus miraculously feeding five thousand people in the wilderness (Mark 6:32–44; Matt. 14:13–21; Luke 9:10–17) alludes to Israel's period in the wilderness following the exodus from Egypt under the leadership of Moses. There, where there was no food, the Israelites were nourished by God, who fed them with *manna,* a mysterious breadlike substance that fell from the sky each morning like dew. The story of Jesus feeding the five thousand makes the points that Jesus was one "like Moses" or even greater than Moses, that his ministry was an act of deliverance parallel in significance to the event that first created Israel, and that the people of God were once again being fed by "supernatural food" in the wilderness.

The story not only points backward to the exodus but also forward to the early church's sacred meal, in which the bread of the Eucharist (or Lord's Supper or Communion or Mass, as the meal is variously known) was understood as the "body of Christ." The bread of the Eucharist is like the manna in the wilderness, the "supernatural food" whereby the people of God are nourished. Indeed, the author of John's Gospel made the connection explicit. At the conclusion of John's story of the feeding of the five thousand (6:1–14), the Jesus of John says, "I am the bread of life," "the bread of God which comes down from heaven and gives life to the world" (6:35, 33). That is, the story ends by saying that *Jesus* (and not the loaves themselves) is the bread in the wilderness, the bread of life.

The modern scholarly approach has thus led to the realization that many of the miracle stories have a *symbolic* thrust. The word "symbolic" makes some Christians uncomfortable, for they tend to hear it as a watering down of the "literal" or "historical." Moreover, there is a modern prejudice against the symbolic, as when we say about something, "It's *only* symbolic," implying that it need therefore not be taken seriously. But to say that a story has symbolic elements is to say that the language or content *points beyond itself* to a web of meanings or associations, and those associations enrich rather than impoverish the story.

Yet it is also true that at this level of interpretation, the historical question is not important. That is, one can write a powerful exposition of the feeding of the five thousand without even addressing the question of its historical actuality; for Christians, Jesus *is* the bread of life who nourishes them again and again with his body and blood, and this is true independently of whatever happened or did not happen on a particular day during his ministry. Though the recognition that a narrative is symbolic need not involve a denial that it is also historical, the historical question is not central. Indeed, within much of modern scholarship, it is often left unaddressed or declared to be unimportant.

The modern scholarly approach is based on a solid insight: the miracle stories are part of the church's story of Jesus, and the meaning of the stories is greatly enhanced by paying attention to the meanings seen by the early church and the allusions they make. Yet the "mighty deeds" of Jesus are also part of *the history of Jesus,* and not simply part of the church's *story about Jesus*. That is, the tradition that Jesus was a "wonder-worker" is historically very firmly attested. Thus, as we move to the miracle stories themselves, we will find it most helpful to divide our treatment into two categories: the miracles as part of the *history of Jesus,* those we can say with reasonable historical probability "really happened," and as part of the *story of Jesus,* those about which we must say, "Perhaps it happened, but the *meaning* of the story seems to lie elsewhere."

The Miracles as Part of the History of Jesus

Mediators between the two worlds of the primordial tradition often become "people of power," or miracle workers, especially healers. To be sure, not all do. In the history of Israel and other cultures, some were primarily mediators of the divine will as prophets and lawgivers or of "supernatural" knowledge as diviners or clairvoyants. Others were charismatic military leaders, "spirit warriors." But some became channels through which healing power flowed from the world of Spirit into the visible world. Such figures of power ("men of deeds," as they were called in Judaism) were known in first-century Palestine, both in its ancient tradition (notably Elijah) and in charismatics contemporary with Jesus such as Hanina ben Dosa and Honi the Circle-Drawer.

Jesus as Healer and Exorcist

Jesus was one of these "men of deeds." Indeed, to his contemporaries, it was the most remarkable thing about him. During his lifetime he was known primarily as a healer and exorcist. People flocked to him, drawn by his wonder-working reputation, as the Gospels report again and again: "They brought to him all who were sick or possessed with demons. And the whole city was gathered around the door" (Mark 1:32–33); "His fame spread . . . and great crowds followed him" (Matt. 4:24–25); "People came to him from every quarter" (Mark 1:45).

His healings attracted attention in other quarters as well. In prison before his execution by King Herod Antipas, John the Baptist heard of Jesus's mighty deeds and sent messengers to inquire if Jesus might be Elijah *returned,* one of the great charismatic healers of Israel's history (Matt. 11:3; Luke 7:19).[2] After John's death, Herod himself heard of Jesus's reputation as a miracle worker and wondered if Jesus's powers might be the powers of John the

Baptist "raised from the dead" (Mark 6:14–15). Not only do the Gospel writers report the fame that Jesus's mighty deeds caused, but they devote substantial portions of their narratives to accounts of such deeds.[3]

Despite the difficulty that miracles pose for the modern mind, on historical grounds it is virtually indisputable that Jesus was a healer and exorcist. The reasons for this judgment are threefold. First, there is the widespread attestation in our earliest sources. Second, healings and exorcisms were relatively common in the world around Jesus, both within Judaism and in the Hellenistic world. Third, even his opponents did not challenge the claim that powers of healing flowed through him; rather, as we shall see, they claimed that his powers came from the lord of the evil spirits. By admiring followers and skeptical foes alike, he was seen as a holy man with healing powers.

True, the accounts in their present form are the product of the Gospel writers. Symbolic and stylistic elements are often present; many details are obviously omitted (the stories are very compact); most often, we cannot be certain that we are dealing with eyewitness reports of particular healings, even when personal names are mentioned. But the stories reflect the *kinds* of situations Jesus encountered and the *kinds* of deeds he did, even if we cannot be sure whether a particular story is a stylized "typical" picture or based fairly closely on eyewitness reports of a specific event. That is, the verdict that we are dealing with generally historical material does not imply the historical accuracy of all details.

Exorcisms

As an exorcist, Jesus drove evil spirits out of many possessed people. In addition to summaries that mention multiple exorcisms (e.g., "And those who were troubled with unclean spirits were cured," Luke 6:18) and the reference to Mary Magdalene "from whom seven demons had gone out" (8:2), the synoptic Gospels contain several extended accounts of particular exorcisms and a number of sayings referring to the practice. The Gospels consistently distinguish between exorcisms and healings; not all healings were exorcisms, and not all maladies were caused by evil spirits. The Gospels also speak of exorcists other than Jesus: Pharisaic exorcists, an unnamed exorcist who expelled demons in Jesus's name even though he was not a follower of Jesus, and Jesus's own disciples.[4] Obviously well attested, exorcisms were not uncommon, even though they were not everyday occurrences.

More so than extraordinary cures, exorcism is especially alien to us in the modern world. In part, this is because we do not normally see the phenomenon (though are there cases of "possession" we call by another name?). Even more, it is because the notion of "possession" by a spirit from another level of reality does not fit into our worldview. Rather, possession and exorcism presuppose the reality of a world of spirits that can interact with the visible world; that is, they presuppose the truth of the "primordial tradition."

Cross-cultural studies of the phenomenon indicate a number of typical traits. "Possession" occurs when a person falls under the control of an evil spirit or spirits. Such people are inhabited by a presence that they (and others) experience as "other than themselves." In addition to having two or more "personalities," they exhibit bizarre behavior and are often destructive or self-destructive. Convulsions, sweating, and seizures are common. Unusual strength and uncanny knowledge are sometimes also reported.[5] Exorcism is the expulsion of the evil spirit, driving it out of the person and ending its "ownership." This can be done only with the aid of a superior spirit in order to overpower the evil spirit. Often elaborate rituals are used, involving incantations and "power objects."[6]

The synoptic Gospels describe two cases of possession in considerable detail. Inhabited by a legion of demons with supernatural strength, the "Gerasene demoniac" lived howling in a graveyard on the eastern shore of the Sea of Galilee:

> A man . . . with an unclean spirit . . . lived among the tombs; and no one could restrain him any more, even with a chain; for he had often been restrained with shackles and chains, but the chains he wrenched apart, and the shackles he broke in pieces; and no one had the strength to subdue him. Night and day among the tombs and on the mountains he was always howling, and bruising himself with stones. . . . Then Jesus asked him, "What is your name?" He replied "My name is Legion; for we are many." (Mark 5:2–5, 9)

According to Mark's account, the demon also had non-ordinary knowledge. It recognized Jesus's "status," even though no human being in Mark's Gospel had yet done so: "What have you to do with me, Jesus, Son of the Most High God?" (5:7).[7]

The self-destructive quality of the Gerasene demoniac is also found in Mark's picture of a demon-possessed boy (9:17–27). Whenever the evil spirit seized him, it dashed him to the ground, causing him to foam at the mouth, grind his teeth, and become rigid; it "often cast him into the fire and into the water, to destroy him."[8]

Typically, Jesus exorcised evil spirits by verbal command alone, as in Mark's report of an exorcism in the synagogue at Capernaum in Galilee (1:23–27).[9] In this case, nothing is said about the condition of the possessed person beyond the presence of more than one "personality" and the recognition by the unclean spirit of the identity of Jesus, as if through nonordinary knowledge. The exorcism itself is accompanied by a convulsion and loud cries. Striking, however, is the reaction of the crowd. Amazed, the people exclaim, "What is this? A new teaching—with authority! He commands even the unclean spirits." Their exclamation suggests what they (or the Gospel writer) saw as the source of Jesus's power to cast out demons: "with *authority* he commands even the unclean spirits," that is, from the mouth of the *Gevurah* (Spirit) he casts out demons.[10]

How modern medical doctors or psychiatrists might diagnose the condition of "possession" or describe the process of exorcism, were they to witness either, is difficult to say. Within the framework of the modern worldview, we are inclined to see "possession" as a primitive prescientific diagnosis of a condition that must have another explanation. Most likely, we would see it as a psychopathological condition that includes among its symptoms the delusion of believing one's self to be possessed. Perhaps a psychopathological diagnosis and explanation are possible.[11] Social conditions also seem to be a factor; there are some data from anthropology and social psychology that suggest that conditions of political oppression, social deprivation, and rapid social change (all of which characterized first-century Palestine) are correlated with increased frequency of possession.[12]

But whatever the modern explanation might be and however much psychological or social factors might be involved, it must be stressed that Jesus and his contemporaries (along with people in most cultures) thought that people could be possessed or inhabited by a spirit or spirits from another plane. Their worldview took for granted the actual existence of such spirits.[13] Perhaps the shared convictions were in part responsible for the phenomenon. In any case, they did not simply *think* of these as cases of possession and exorcism; rather, all of the participants—possessed, exorcist, onlookers—*experienced* the event as an exorcism of a spiritual force that had taken possession of the person.

Jesus's exorcisms not only attracted crowds, but also controversy. Some of his opponents charged that he performed them with the aid of evil powers: "And the scribes who came down from Jerusalem said, 'He has Beelzebul, and by the ruler of the demons he casts out demons'" (Mark 3:22).[14] The accusation was "witchcraft" or "sorcery."[15] A Jewish source from a few centuries later, referring to Jesus by his name in Aramaic, repeated the charge and connected it to his death: "Yeshu of Nazareth" was executed "because he *practiced sorcery* and led Israel astray."[16] The charge of sorcery is a pejorative characterization of his powers and attributes them (like the Beelzebul accusation) to the powers of darkness. From his opponents' point of view, he was an unorthodox holy man, a "magician,"[17] but his powers were not denied.

Jesus responded to the accusation by affirming that the power flowing through him was the Spirit of God: "If it is by *the Spirit of God* that I cast out demons, then the kingdom of God has come to you" (Matt. 12:28; Luke 11:20). Indeed, Jesus saw his exorcisms as a sign that the "strong man" whom he had watched fall from heaven (Luke 10:18) had been "bound" and overcome by the Spirit of God: "But no one can enter a strong man's house and plunder his property without first tying up the strong man; then indeed the house may be plundered" (Mark 3:27). Thus Jesus's exorcisms, as well as his opponents' accusations, link him unmistakably to the thought world and experiential world of the Spirit-filled charismatic. He was one who experienced the Spirit of God flowing through him with power.

Healings

Jesus was also known as a healer. In fact, according to the Gospels, his healings outnumbered his exorcisms. They are often referred to in summary statements[18] as well as in words attributed to Jesus himself. To messengers sent to him by John the Baptist, he said, "Go and tell John what you hear and see: the blind receive their sight, the lame walk, the lepers are cleansed, the deaf hear, the dead are raised, and the poor have good news brought to them" (Matt. 11:4–5; Luke 7:22).[19]

In addition to these summaries, the synoptic Gospels contain thirteen narratives of healings of particular conditions: fever (Mark 1:29–31), leprosy (Mark 1:40–45; Luke 17:11–19), paralysis (Mark 2:1–12), withered hand (Mark 3:1–6), bent back (Luke 13:10–17), hemorrhage (Mark 5:24–34), deafness and dumbness (Mark 7:37), blindness (Mark 8:22–26, 10:46–52), dropsy (Luke 14:1–6), severed ear (Luke 22:51), and a sickness near death or paralysis (Luke 7:1–10; Matt. 8:5–13). These thirteen should not be thought of as the sum total of Jesus's healings; rather, they are narrated as "typical" or to make some point or other. Given the nature of the Gospel narratives, we shall not treat the question of the precise event behind each account, but will simply note the impression the stories create. Even though we are not dealing with "newspaper account" material, we are at the very least in touch with how Jesus's very early followers, still in contact with the living oral tradition, "saw" him.

The stories create a vivid impression of a charismatic healer at work. Sometimes Jesus healed by word. He said to the man with the withered hand, "Stretch out your hand," and the hand was restored (Mark 3:5). Most often touching was also involved. When a leper came to him, Jesus was "moved with pity" and touched him, and immediately the leprosy left him (1:40–42). Sometimes he used physical means in addition to touching, as in the case of a deaf man. Jesus "put his fingers into his ears, and he spat and touched his tongue. Then looking up to heaven, he sighed and said to him, 'Ephphatha,' that is, 'Be opened.' And immediately his ears were opened, his tongue was released, and he spoke plainly" (7:32–35)[20] Of special interest here is the Aramaic word *ephphatha,* "Be opened." In context, it clearly refers to the opening of the man's ears, but may also have the connotation of *the heavens* opening up: "Looking up to heaven, he said, 'Be opened.'" Through the opening in heaven, healing power flowed.

Like the contemporary Galilean holy man Hanina ben Dosa, Jesus healed at a distance. A Roman centurion entreated Jesus to heal his servant who was lying paralyzed in the centurion's home some distance away. Seeing the centurion's faith, Jesus said, "Go; let it be done for you according to your faith." The text concludes: "And the servant [at home] was healed in that hour" (Matt. 8:13).

To attempt to explain how these happened is beyond our purpose, and probably impossible. There is a tendency to see these as "faith healings," perhaps because doing so makes possible a psychosomatic explanation that stretches but does not break the limits of the modern worldview. But, though faith is involved in some of the stories, clearly in other cases the faith of the healed person was not involved at all.

Rather, within the thought world of the accounts themselves, Jesus's healings were the result of "power." Indeed, the favorite word for the mighty deeds of Jesus in the synoptic Gospels is, in Greek, *dunamis,* which translates as "power." It is most frequently used in the plural—the mighty deeds of Jesus were "powers." It is sometimes used in the singular to refer to one of the central qualities of God: "the *power* of God" or "the *power* of the Most High." It can even be used as a name for God: "And you will see the Son of Man seated at the right hand of *the Power*" (Mark 14:62). That is, the deeds of Jesus were understood by the Gospel writers and Jesus himself as *powers* from *the Power.*

In the book of Acts, written by Luke and therefore also reflecting a synoptic point of view, this power is directly associated with the Spirit of God: "But you will receive *power* when the Holy Spirit has come upon you" (1:8). Luke also makes the connection in his Gospel: "Then Jesus, filled with *the power of the Spirit,* returned to Galilee" (4:14). Thus, from the standpoint of the Gospels, the mighty deeds of Jesus, exorcisms and healings alike, were the product of the power that flowed through him as a holy man. His powers were charismatic, the result of his having become a channel for the power of the other realm, what Jesus and his contemporaries also called Spirit.

The Miracles as Part of the Story of Jesus

In addition to exorcisms and healings, the synoptic Gospels report a number of other "spectacular" deeds: two resuscitations of apparently dead people (Mark 5:21–24, 35–43; Luke 7:11–17); two sea miracles (stilling a storm, Mark 4:35–41, and walking on the sea, 6:45–52); two feeding miracles (the feeding of the five thousand, Mark 6:30–44, and the feeding of the four thousand, 8:1–10); a "miraculous" catch of fish (Luke 5:1–11); and the "cursing" and "withering" of a fig tree (Mark 11:12–14, 20–25).[21] Are these narratives to be taken historically? Did Jesus also do these kinds of things? Two factors make it very difficult to know.

First, we simply do not know if there are limits to the powers of a charismatic mediator. For example, are resuscitations of *genuinely* dead people possible? Or, alternatively, does levitation really happen, and might walking on water be a special case of levitation? That is, the historical verdict about whether or not such events really happened will depend in part upon whether we think even a charismatic can do things like this.[22]

Second, symbolic elements abound in these narratives. The points of correspondence between these stories and the literary-religious tradition of the early church are so frequent and pronounced that perhaps the narratives as a whole (and not just details within them) are to be understood primarily or only in terms of how they point beyond themselves rather than historically at all.[23] As we have noted, doing so does not *require* a negative historical judgment; a narrative with symbolic elements can have a historical nucleus. But we will find it most illuminating to consider the stories of these "other powers" as part of the church's story about Jesus and not primarily as part of the history of Jesus himself.

Classic among these are the feeding stories and the stories of Jesus stilling the storm and walking on the water. In an important sense, neither of the sea stories concerns the public ministry of Jesus; rather, only his inner group of followers is present. In both stories, they are in a boat, at night, distressed and frightened; in both, Jesus comes to them, the winds cease, and the sea is calmed.

Central to these stories is the "sea," an image that reverberates with rich resonances of meaning in the Hebrew Bible. The Hebrew word for "sea," derived from the name of the evil god in the Babylonian creation story, carried connotations of evil and was a mysterious and threatening force opposed to God. Accordingly, when the ancient Hebrews wanted to stress God's power and authority, they spoke of the divine mastery over the sea. The authors of Psalms exclaimed, "The sea is his, for he made it" (95:5) and "You rule the raging of the sea; when its waves rise, you still them" (89:9). According to the book of Job, it was God who "shut in the sea with doors" and said to it, "Thus far shall you come, and no farther, and here shall your proud waves be stopped" (38:8, 11).

The plight of the disciples and their cry for help echo another passage from Psalms that describes people in a storm at sea:

> *For he commanded and raised the stormy wind,*
> > *which lifted up the waves of the sea.*
> *They mounted up to heaven, they went down to the depths;*
> > *their courage melted away in their calamity;*
> *they reeled and staggered like drunkards,*
> > *and were at their wits' end.*
> *Then they cried to the LORD in their trouble,*
> > *and he brought them out from their distress;*
> *he made the storm be still,*
> > *and the waves of the sea were hushed.* (107:25–29)

These connections to language and imagery that were part of the early church's literary-religious tradition suggest that the story is to be understood within that larger framework.

Putting all of these elements together, the narrative makes several points. The picture of Jesus stilling the storm makes the claim that he shares in the power and authority of God; what was said of God in the Old Testament is now said of Jesus. Moreover, like the Lord of the psalm narrative, he responds to his followers' cry of distress when the forces of evil and chaos threaten to overwhelm them. Finally, a boat was one of the images for the early church, perhaps by the time Mark's narrative was written. If Mark was making use of this image, then the narrative portrays Jesus as the Lord of the church who saves his people when they turn to him for help in distress. The cry of the disciples is the church's cry, "Lord save us! We are perishing!" (Matt. 8:25), and the words of Jesus to the disciples are addressed to the church: "Take heart, it is I; do not be afraid" (Mark 6:50). In short, the *purpose* of the narrative may be symbolic rather than historical. Moreover, it is no less *true* for being symbolic; indeed, its truth is verified in the experience of Christians ever since, quite apart from the historical verdict about whether the story describes an actual incident one night on the Sea of Galilee.

Symbolic elements similarly point to a meaning beyond historical reporting in the other "spectacular" narratives. The most sensational of the resuscitation stories, the raising of Lazarus, in John's Gospel (11:1–44), is viewed by scholars as not primarily historical in nature.[24] Of the two synoptic resuscitations, one seems not to have been an actual one, but a "revival" of a person mistakenly thought to be dead, a mistake relatively common prior to modern methods of diagnosis. To the wailing people gathered around the bed of Jairus's daughter, Jesus said, "Why do you make a commotion and weep? The child is *not dead but sleeping*" (Mark 5:39). Whatever one makes of the historicity behind these stories, the accounts have a symbolic edge; namely, the "raising of the dead" was associated with the coming of the "new age" and the Messiah. Thus the accounts may be expressing symbolically the conviction that the new age and the Messiah had come.

Finally, there is another power, rather strange, which Jesus spoke of, even though no story is told of his actually using this power: immunity to poisonous serpents. "See, I have given you authority *to tread on snakes and scorpions,* and over all the power of the enemy; and nothing will hurt you" (Luke 10:19).[25]

Interestingly, the same power was reported of another Jewish holy man, Hanina ben Dosa. While he was praying, "A poisonous snake bit him, but he did not interrupt his prayer." Later, the onlookers found the snake dead at the opening of its hole and exclaimed, "Woe to the man bitten by a snake, but woe to the snake which bites Rabbi Hanina ben Dosa."[26] According to the book of Acts, the apostle Paul enjoyed a similar immunity (28:1–6). Clearly, the "power" links Jesus once again to the charismatic stream of Judaism. But are the words about power over snakes to be understood literally or symbolically, perhaps pointing beyond themselves to power over Satan; or, given the story of the tempter in the Garden of Eden taking the form of a serpent, to power over sin?

Thus, about all of these stories of "other powers" a clear historical judgment is impossible. Moreover, one cannot overcome the historical uncertainty through an act of faith. An account cannot be made historically true by believing it to be so. For example, I may choose to believe that George Washington actually threw a silver dollar across the Potomac, but my belief has nothing to do with whether he actually did; he may or may not have.[27] The same is true with the historical question about whether

Jesus actually did these things. Believing that he did so has nothing to do with whether he actually did. One cannot solve the historical question by faith or belief. In short, the mighty deeds of Jesus other than his exorcisms and healings must remain in a "historical suspense account."[28]

Though one must be uncertain about these stories as part of the history of Jesus, their meanings as part of the church's story of Jesus are clear. Using imagery rich with associations in that time, the stories affirm that the living Christ of the early church's experience was (and for Christians still is) one who, sharing in the power of God, delivered them from peril and evil, nourished them in the wilderness, and brought life out of death.

Conclusion

In their historical context, the miracles of Jesus do not "prove" that he was divine. In the tradition in which he stood, including figures from its ancient past and persons contemporary with him, the healings and exorcisms reported of him were not unique. Yet though the historical study of the miracles results in the loss of their uniqueness, it produces a gain in their credibility. Contrary to the modern notion that such events are impossible, we must grant that the historical evidence that Jesus stood in the stream of Jewish charismatic healers is very strong.

He was, with regard to cultural and historical impact, the most extraordinary figure in that tradition. Not only did he come out of such a stream, but others followed in his wake. According to the Gospels, he commissioned his twelve disciples to be charismatic healers (Mark 6:7–13; Matt. 10:5–8; Luke 10:8–9). His two most important first-century followers, Peter and Paul, were also charismatic holy men. Further removed in time, St. Francis of Assisi (1176–1226), often considered the most "Christlike" of subsequent Christians, was a mystic, visionary, and healer. Though foreign to our experience and way of thinking in the modern world, the world of spirits and God was, for Jesus and his predecessors and followers in the Jewish-Christian tradition, very real—not simply as an element of belief, but of experience.

Chapter 7

Is Jesus God?

A VERY FEW DAYS AGO, I received by e-mail a letter about Jesus from a person who is reading one of my books. His thoughts and questions struck me as being of interest to many people. I quote the letter at length and then share my response.

A Letter About Jesus

Your book has persuaded me that much of the language of the Bible and theology is metaphorical and

---

Originally published on *Patheos.com,* July 12, July 27, and August 19, 2014.

should not be taken literally. Granted that, at what
point do you think one reaches a gray area as to
whether Jesus was even divine?

I believe I'm getting a better sense of your views as I
read, but please correct me if I'm misinterpreting. You
essentially say that many of the Gospel stories should
be taken metaphorically. This, you argue, doesn't imply
that they can't have a rich meaning or even be divinely
inspired (?). In fact, we may derive more meaning from
them by taking a metaphorical/historical approach.

But it does mean that Jesus didn't really do *x, y,* or
z. Clearly you must believe Jesus was divine. Otherwise, why would you be a "Christian"? I think you said
something along the lines of Jesus being the perfect embodiment of what God is like in human form. That's
different from saying that he *was* God, or God incarnate.

So, do you believe he was God? And if so, what has
convinced you? I mean, if the miracle stories are metaphorical (you say he must have been a great healer, but
I think you believe there have been other great healers/
mystics), what are we left with as evidence that he was
more than a man?

He clearly was a revolutionary and a wisdom
teacher, but that doesn't make him more than a man.
You are not convinced that he rose in bodily form,
which is fine. But is it not just a small step to go from
saying that he was "experienced" in some way after
his death to saying he didn't appear at all?

Are we placing the idea of his divinity solely on these "experiences" of him, if we aren't taking the miracle stories or the bodily resurrection literally? As a side note, what if it's possible for other people's spirits to appear after death—ordinary people who pass on to a spirit world and aren't divine, but perhaps in very rare occasions can be seen again? Doesn't it leave open the possibility that Jesus was just one of these and not God incarnate?

What has convinced you that he is worthy of being worshipped? Is it the stories of the unshakable belief and devotion by the apostles after his death? And are many of these even credible? (I haven't read enough to know.) Sorry for the length of my epistle.

My Response

To say the obvious, the core of your letter concerns the divinity of Jesus. About that there's more than one thing to say.

Was Jesus God? No. Not even the New Testament says that. It speaks of him as the Word of God, the Son of God, the Messiah, and so forth, but never simply identifies or equates him with God. As John's Gospel puts it, he is the Word become flesh—that is, he reveals what can be seen of God in a finite human life. To say, "I believe Jesus was God" (as some Christians do, or think they are supposed to) goes beyond what the New Testament affirms and is thus more than biblical. He is the Word incarnate—not the disembodied Word.

Did some of his followers experience Jesus as a divine reality after his death, and have some Christians had such experiences in the centuries since, including into the present? Yes. These experiences led to the conviction that Jesus was "one with God" or "at the right hand of God" and ultimately to the doctrine of the Trinity: that God is one (monotheism) and yet known/experienced in three primary ways (as God, the Son, and the Spirit). This is the context in which it makes sense to praise and pray to Jesus. But this doesn't mean that Jesus of Nazareth, Jesus during his historical life, was "God."

Jesus of Nazareth was completely human. He did not have a divine component that made him different in kind from the rest of us. That's what it means to say he was "true man," "fully human." He didn't have a divine supercharger.

Does that make him ordinary? No. I think he is one of the two most remarkable human beings who ever lived. I don't really care who the other one was—my point is that what we see in Jesus is a human possibility. That's what makes him so remarkable. If he was also divine, then he's not all that remarkable. If he had the knowledge and power of God, he could have done so much more.

Christian language about the exalted status of Jesus—as the Word of God, the Son of God, the Messiah, and so forth—is testimony, witness: this is who Jesus became and who he is in Christian experience, life, and thought. This is who he is for those of us who are Christians.

Further Thoughts on a Letter About Jesus

My previous blog—"A Letter About Jesus"—drew a much larger response than I expected. In this blog, I continue that conversation with a clarification and some additional comments.

Clarification—even as I think this was pretty clear in my previous blog. One of my major claims was that the New Testament does not simply identify and equate Jesus and God. It never says, "Jesus is God" or "God is Jesus."

Of course, it does affirm, in phrases from John's Gospel, that Jesus is the "Word of God" and "one with God." But that does not mean that Jesus was God. Rather, in John's language, he was the "Word become flesh." He revealed what can be seen of God in a human life—and that means within the limitations of human life.

To affirm that Jesus is the Word become flesh, the Word incarnate, means what another New Testament verse does: he is "the image (*ikon*) of the invisible God" (Col. 1:15). He shows us what God is like—reveals God's character and passion.

But none of this means that the New Testament teaches that Jesus was God—as if all of God was in Jesus during his historical life. To use the language of the Trinity, God the Father did not cease to be while Jesus was alive. Jesus was "God's Son," not God the Father. Was the Son like the Father? Yes. Was the Son the Father during the life of Jesus? No. Are they in an important and complex sense one? Yes. But to equate God and Jesus during his historical lifetime is bad history and bad theology. It is the product of precritical conventional and uncritical dogmatic Christian thinking. Sounds harsh. But think about it.

An additional comment. The conflict among Christians about whether or not Jesus was God is grounded in two different understandings of the Gospels—and the New Testament and the Bible as a whole. One view—generally embraced by "conservative" Christians—sees the Bible and the Gospels as "divine information." That is shorthand for the view that the Bible and the Gospels are the direct revelation of God and thus have a divine guarantee to be true. For them, divine inspiration means divine inerrancy.

A second view sees the Gospels as the product of a historical process, written in a particular time and setting. Time: the earliest was probably written around 70, the last perhaps as late as the early second century. Setting: they are the product of early Christian communities, written from within and to those communities. As such, they combine early Christian *memory* of Jesus and *testimony* about Jesus: their memories of what he was like, of what he taught and did, and their testimony to what he had become in their experience and lives, his significance for them.

To illustrate the difference generated by these two ways of seeing the Gospels, reflect upon the series of "I am" statements attributed to Jesus in John (and only John). In them, Jesus refers to himself as "the Light of the World," "the Bread of Life," "the Door," "the Good Shepherd," "the Resurrection and the Life," "the Way, the Truth, and the Life," and "the Vine." For the first view, this is "divine information"—the direct revelation of God about who Jesus is. And because John says Jesus said this about himself, that means that he did.

The second way of seeing the Gospels understands this language as early Christian testimony to Jesus and not as memory of what Jesus said about himself. A major reason for this verdict is that the first three Gospels (the synoptic Gospels, Matthew, Mark, and Luke) do not report that Jesus said anything like this about himself. Within this way of seeing the Gospels, the "I am" statements in John are best understood if we turn them into third-person statements about Jesus: Jesus is "the Light of the World," "the Bread of Life," "the Way, the Truth, and the Life," and so forth. This is the testimony of the Christian community within which and for which John was written.

As a concluding illustration of the difference made by the interconnected issues of whether we think Jesus was God and how we see the Gospels, I suggest the miracle stories of Jesus and the sea (Mark 4:35–41; 6:45–52). They share in common that the disciples are in mortal peril in a boat on a stormy sea. Jesus rescues them by stilling the tempest. He comes to them walking on the sea.

Those who think of Jesus as God and the Gospels as divine information hear these stories literally and evidentially.

Anybody who can still a storm at sea and walk on the water must have divine power, indeed be divine, for no mere human could do that. This hearing of the stories sees them as reports of spectacular events that happened in the distant past, long ago and far away. They matter because of what they demonstrate or prove: that Jesus had divine powers, that he was more than human.

Just as the first way of hearing these stories combines a way of seeing Jesus with a way of seeing the Gospels, so does the second. It takes seriously that as a human being, as an incarnate being, Jesus did not have supernatural powers during his historical lifetime. Was he "filled with the Spirit"? Yes. Was he a healer? Yes. But could he change water into wine? Multiply food so that he could feed a multitude of five thousand (or more) with a few loaves and fishes? For this way of seeing Jesus, he was a vulnerable human being living within the conditions of finitude, incarnation. He was born and could be (and was) killed. He was not God, but the revelation of what can be seen of God in a human life.

Within this framework, the miracles on the sea are not historical data proving that Jesus was God. They are about what trust in Jesus and God produce. Jesus stills the storms that threaten us. He makes it possible to walk on the water, the void, the abyss, without sinking.

Within the Gospels, this metaphorical—more-than-literal—meaning is clearly intended. As Matthew takes over the story from Mark of Jesus walking on the water, he adds an episode. Peter also walks on the water—

successfully. But then he becomes afraid and begins to sink (Matt. 14:22–33). The story identifies Peter's fear with "little faith." With faith, we can walk on water. Literally? No. The story is about the importance of trusting in Jesus. It is about faith as trust, the opposite of fear. It is about the significance of Jesus, not about something he once did.

A final reflection question: What is added to the story of Jesus by thinking that he was God and therefore could do spectacular deeds that no one else could or can? Does his story gain meaning? Or is something lost? Was Jesus extraordinary because he was God? Or was he extraordinary because he was an utterly remarkable human being, one of us?

Postscript to a Letter About Jesus

This is my third installment about "A Letter About Jesus" and the issue "Was Jesus God?" If you have not read the first two installments, this may not make much sense to you.

To emphasize: as a Christian, I affirm that Jesus is the "Word of God" and the "Word become flesh," that is, the Word incarnate, the Word embodied in a human life. In Jesus, we see what can be seen of God in a human life. This affirmation goes back to the first Christian century and is orthodox Christianity.

For those who want to say more than "Jesus is the Word embodied in a human being," namely, that "Jesus was God," a challenge: What do you mean? Do you mean that Jesus as a historical person had the mind and power of God—that he was omniscient as God is commonly thought to be? And that he had divine powers—that like God he was omnipotent and could do anything? And if you don't mean that, what do you mean?

If what you mean is that Jesus as the Word of God embodied in a human life is the decisive revelation of what can be seen of God in a human life (namely, God's character and what God is passionate about), then our disagreement may be about words rather than substance. But if you mean more than that, what do you mean?

Finally, I recognize that for some Christians, Jesus has become one of the names of God. People praise and pray to Jesus. I have no problem with that—unless that is projected back on the historical Jesus so that he becomes superhuman and thus not one of us. The Word become flesh—the incarnation—means that he was one of us.

Chapter 8

Taking Jesus Seriously

MYSTIC, WISDOM TEACHER, SOCIAL PROPHET

I BEGIN WITH THE IMPORTANCE of distinguishing between the historical Jesus and the risen, living Christ, between the pre-Easter Jesus and the post-Easter Jesus. When I was young, growing up in the church, I didn't make this distinction. I didn't know about it and perhaps couldn't have made it even if I had heard about it. As a result, I saw Jesus as more divine than human. That is because I lumped everything together that I heard about Jesus from

---

Sermon delivered at Calvary Episcopal Church, Memphis, Tennessee, as part of the Lenten Noonday Preaching Series, March 17, 1997.

the Gospels, Christian preaching, and Christian hymns, creeds, and so forth. Hence, I thought of him, even as a historical figure, as already having the mind of God and the power of God. Because I thought of him as more divine than human, I really lost track of the utterly remarkable human being that he was.

South African Jesus scholar Albert Nolan makes the same point when he says in a quotation that I've grown very fond of: "Jesus is a much underrated man. When we deprive him of his humanity, we deprive him of his greatness." This leads me to state the premise or the starting point for my sermon today, which is the classic and traditional Christian affirmation about Jesus, namely, that Jesus is for us as Christians the decisive revelation of what a life full of God is like. I see this claim as the central meaning of the Christological language of the New Testament. The human Jesus is the Word made flesh. The human Jesus is the wisdom of God. The human Jesus is the Spirit of God embodied in human life. In short, the meaning of all the statements about Jesus show us what a life full of God is like.

So what was Jesus like? I'm going to begin by providing you with my most compact summary of the historical Jesus, a threefold summary. For those of you who know my books, this will be very familiar, but it is also very compact so, hopefully, not too tedious.

I speak of Jesus first of all as a *Jewish mystic*. By this I mean that Jesus is one who knew God, who knew the sacred, who knew the Spirit—terms I use synonymously and interchangeably. He was one for whom the Spirit of God was an experiential reality.

Second, I see the historical Jesus as a *wisdom teacher*. As a wisdom teacher, he was a teacher of a way or a path. I speak about that way or that path with four short sentences, all of which I understand to be saying the same thing. It was a way that led beyond convention. It was the road less traveled—to use a phrase we know from M. Scott Peck, who in turn borrowed it from Robert Frost. It was, to use language from Jesus himself, the narrow way, the narrow gate. The contrast is to the broad way of conventional wisdom. Fourth, and finally, it was a subversive and alternative wisdom.

The third statement in my threefold summary of what the historical Jesus was like is that he was a *social prophet*. As a social prophet, he was like the great social prophets of the Hebrew Bible or the Old Testament—people who also had vivid experiences of God and who in the name of God became God-intoxicated voices of socioreligious protest directed against the domination systems of their day. These domination systems were marked by an economics of exploitation and a politics of oppression and were legitimated most frequently with a religious ideology, legitimated in the name of God. Jesus was like them—a radical critic of the domination system in the Jewish homeland in his day. Indeed, it was his passion as a social prophet that accounts for his getting killed. This is the political meaning of Good Friday. To put that threefold summary into three phases, there was to Jesus, first, a Spirit dimension, second, a wisdom dimension, and, third, a justice dimension.

Now, what would it mean to take a figure like this, namely Jesus, seriously as a disclosure or a revelation of what a life full of God is like? What do we see? What would such a life look like? I will speak about this again with the same three subheadings I have just named. First, it would be a life lived *in relationship to* the same *Spirit* that Jesus knew in his own experience. It would mean that the Christian life would not be very much about believing, and would not be about believing for the sake of heaven later; it is about the transforming relationship with God in the present. Indeed, I see this to be the central meaning of spirituality.

Spirituality I define as becoming conscious of and intentional about our relationship to God. I say "conscious of," because I firmly maintain that we are all already in a relationship with God and we have been so since our very beginning, whether we know that or not, believe that or not. Spirituality is about becoming conscious of that relationship. I say "intentional," because I see spirituality as being about paying attention to that relationship, being intentional about deepening that relationship and letting that relationship grow. Just as human relationships grow and deepen through spending time in them and paying attention to them, so also our relationship with God grows in this same way.

Second, a life that takes Jesus seriously as a disclosure of what a life full of God is like would be a life lived by *the alternative wisdom of Jesus.* The alternative wisdom of Jesus, the way less traveled, is in fact the same as a life lived in relationship to the Spirit. The wisdom of Jesus leads us into a radical centering in the sacred, in God. The contrast is to the life of conventional wisdom, which is the life that most of us live most of the time. I want to call your attention to two of the many consequences of living in the world of conventional wisdom. The first is that conventional wisdom blinds us to wonder.

Let me move into this by explaining briefly what conventional wisdom is. Conventional wisdom is a culture's most taken-for-granted notions about two things—about *what is real* and about *how to live.* Conventional wisdom is cultural consensus. Conventional wisdom is what everybody knows, and it is what we are socialized into as we grow up. Growing up is basically learning the categories, labels, and language of your culture. These categories and labels form a grid that gets imposed on reality, and the effect of this blinds us to the wondrous reality in which we live.

Let me try to illustrate this in a very simple way. Imagine that you had never before in your life seen a four-legged furry creature and then you see a cat. You would be utterly fascinated by that. Your attention would be riveted on that cat. Because cats are familiar to us and because we have the word "cat," most often when we see a cat, a little label goes on in our head that says "cat," and we don't pay any more attention to it unless it is an especially striking cat, we've got a lot of time on our hands, or it is our cat. The point is that conventional wisdom blinds us to the sheer wonder of what is. It makes things look ordinary and familiar and nothing special.

When you think about it, the real wonder, in a way, is that this could ever look ordinary to us. You know how remarkable it is that we are, and that there is anything, and that we are here, and that this is all around us. Yet conventional wisdom reduces reality to the visible world of our ordinary experience, which is nothing special. This is the secular form of conventional wisdom. There is a religious form of conventional wisdom as well. The religious form of conventional wisdom with its excessive certitude blinds us to the mystery and wonder of life.

A second effect of conventional wisdom is that it tells us how to live. It gets embedded within our minds as we grow up—the central values of our culture. One could make a very good case that the central values of modern Western culture are centered in what I have called the three As—appearance, affluence, and achievement. All of us, at least in the first half of our lives, are to a large extent driven by these values. Driven by these values, we become blind to much else as well as burdened and preoccupied with how we measure up to those values of appearance, affluence, and achievement. The way of Jesus is an invitation out of that kind of life—an invitation into a radically different kind of life.

To put it abstractly, the wisdom teaching of Jesus invites us to a radical decentering and recentering, a decentering from that world of conventional wisdom and a recentering in the Spirit of God. To put it less abstractly by using one of the familiar images or metaphors of the New Testament, the way of Jesus involves dying to an old way of being and being born into a new way of being. That death and rebirth are at the very center of the Christian life.

This way of Jesus has as its central fruit growth in compassion; delivered from the blinders of conventional wisdom, we become more compassionate beings. We see the wondrous creature that each of us is. We are also delivered from the preoccupation with pursuing the values of our culture that beat like a drum in our heads.

The third element in my threefold summary is what I want to highlight in this sermon, because it is the most unfamiliar and most unsettling to us. It is the *justice* dimension of taking Jesus seriously. The God of the Bible, as we see that God disclosed in Moses, the prophets, and Jesus, is passionate about justice, about social justice, not about criminal justice. Why this passion for justice? Why is the God of the Bible so passionate about justice? The answer, it seems to me, is disarmingly simple. Because God cares about human suffering, and the single greatest source of unnecessary human suffering, of unnecessary social misery, is systemic injustice. By systemic injustice I mean sources of suffering caused by cultural systems, by the structures of society. I think in many ways, this is a difficult notion for us, made more difficult to grasp by the ethos of American individualism.

So let me say a bit more about systemic injustice. Think of all the suffering caused throughout history in the ancient world and in the contemporary world by economic exploitation and destructive impoverishment, by the way elites in every society have made the system work in their own self-interest, by political oppression, by all the isms—racism, sexism, nationalism, imperialism, and you can add your own isms. These are all examples of systemic injustice. Injustice is built into cultural systems. More subtly, think of all the suffering caused by rigidly held convention and the cultural shaming that frequently goes along with it.

Jesus as a social prophet, in the tradition of the great social prophets of Israel, stood against the systemic injustice of his day. Taking Jesus seriously means that our own consciousness needs to be raised regarding the way in which cultural systems cause enormous suffering for people. We need to understand that the ethical imperative that flows from Jesus is both personal and political. It is both compassion and justice. So to sum this up, taking Jesus seriously means a life increasingly centered in the Spirit of God, a life lived by the alternative wisdom of Jesus, and a life marked by compassion and justice.

To move to my conclusion, I want to relate all of this to the word "repent." "Repent" is one of those very heavy words. When I was growing up, repenting was always associated with experiencing guilt and becoming really contrite about one's sinfulness. (Here I think of a remark made by one of my colleagues, John Dominic Crossan, about a week ago. It is one of those wonderful remarks that he makes so often. He said that he thinks of guilt on the heart as like gas on the stomach—something to be gotten rid of, a flatulence of consciousness, if you will.)

The roots of the word "repent" are very interesting and suggest something quite different—not intensification of guilt and contrition. When we look at the Greek roots of the word "repentance," the verb is *metanoata*. The noun is *metanoia*. *Meta* means "beyond." The noun from which the second part of the word "repent" is derived is *nous* in Greek, and it means "mind." Putting that together, "to repent" means "to go beyond the mind that you have."

We are invited to go beyond the minds that we have to minds and hearts that are shaped by the Spirit of God. We are invited to go beyond the minds that we have—minds dominated and blinded by conventional categories, identities, and preoccupations—to minds and hearts centered in the Spirit, alive to wonder, alive to seeing, and alive to compassion. We are invited to go beyond the minds that we have—minds dominated by the ideologies and preoccupations of individualism—to minds and hearts that see and hear the suffering caused by systemic injustice, to minds alive to God's passion for justice.

All of this, it seems to me, is what it means to take Jesus seriously. The path of following Jesus is an invitation to go beyond the minds that we have.

Chapter 9

Stand with Jesus

So what does it mean to stand with Jesus? What does it mean to take him seriously? What does it mean to follow him?

Drawing upon my study of the historical Jesus, of the pre-Easter Jesus, it seems to me that a life that takes Jesus seriously would have two primary focal points, and that is what I want to talk about today.

The first of these focal points of the Christian life is *a life deeply centered in God,* deeply centered in the

Sermon delivered at Calvary Episcopal Church, Memphis, Tennessee, as part of the Lenten Noonday Preaching Series, March 15, 2001.

Spirit. God or the Spirit was at the very center of Jesus's own life.

In my historical work, I speak of Jesus as a Jewish mystic, and I see this as foundational to everything else that he was. What I mean by the word "mystic" is actually quite simple. Mystics—and they are known in every culture that we know anything about—are people who have vivid and typically frequent experiences of God or the sacred or the Spirit—terms I use synonymously and interchangeably.

The Jewish tradition before Jesus is full of such people. According to the stories told about them, Abraham, Jacob, Moses, and the prophets of ancient Israel were all people for whom God or the sacred was an experiential reality. These people did not simply believe strongly in God; they knew God. Once one takes seriously that there really are people like this, then it seems clear to me that whatever else we say about Jesus, we need to say that he was one of these—one who knew God in his own experience.

If we take Jesus seriously as a Jewish mystic, it also affects how we think about God or the sacred. It means that we need to think about God not as a personlike being out there separate from the universe, a long way away, not here. But it means we need to think of God or the sacred as the encompassing Spirit that is all around us and that is separated from us only by the membranes of our own consciousness. A mystic like Jesus is one in whom those membranes of consciousness become very thin, and one experiences God or the sacred. Jesus invited his followers into a relationship to the same Spirit, the same God that he knew in his own experience.

How do we become centered in the Spirit of God? How do we actually experience what Jesus experienced? Well, the Gospels of the New Testament have many ways of talking about that, about the "way" or the "path." One of the central images for the way or the path is what the journey of Lent itself is about.

The journey of Lent is about journeying with Jesus from Galilee to Jerusalem—which is the place of endings as well as beginnings, the place of death and resurrection. It is the place where, to use an old wordplay, "The tomb becomes a womb."

That journey of Jesus from Galilee to Jerusalem is at the very center of the synoptic Gospels, Matthew, Mark, and Luke. We see it, perhaps, with greatest clarity in Mark's Gospel. Three times in that great central section (8:27–10:52), Jesus speaks of his own impending death and resurrection in Jerusalem. He says, "The Son of Man must undergo great suffering, and be rejected by the elders, the chief priests, and the scribes, and be killed, and after three days rise again" (8:31). After each of those three predictions of the Passion, as they are called, Jesus speaks of following after him, of following him on that path of death and resurrection.

Lent is about precisely that journey. Lent is about mortality and transformation. We begin the season of Lent on Ash Wednesday with the sign of the cross smeared on our foreheads with ashes as the words are spoken over us, "You are dust, and to dust you shall return" (Gen. 3:19).

We begin this season of Lent not only reminded of our death, but also marked for death. The Lenten journey, with its climax in Holy Week and Good Friday and Easter, is about participating in the death and resurrection of Jesus. Put somewhat abstractly, this means dying to an old identity—the identity conferred by culture, by tradition, by parents, perhaps—and being born into a new identity—an identity centered in the Spirit of God. It means dying to an old way of being and being born into a new way of being, a way of being centered once again in God.

Put slightly more concretely, this path of death and resurrection, of radical centering in God, may mean for some of us that we need to die to specific things in our lives—perhaps to a behavior or a pattern of behavior that has become destructive or dysfunctional; perhaps to a relationship that has ended or gone bad; perhaps to an unresolved grief that needs to be let go of; perhaps to a career or job that has either been taken from us or no longer nourishes us; or perhaps even we need to die to a deadness in our lives.

You can even die to deadness, and this dying is oftentimes a daily rhythm in our lives—that daily occurrence that happens to some of us as we remind ourselves of the reality of God in our relationship to God; that reminder that can take us out of ourselves, lift us out of our confinement, take away our feeling of being burdened and weighed down.

So that's the first focal point of a life that takes Jesus seriously: that radical centering in the Spirit of God that is at the very center of the Christian life. Now, this radical centering in God does not leave us unchanged. It transforms us, and this leads us to the second focal point of what it means to follow Jesus, what it means to take Jesus seriously.

In a single sentence, it means compassion in the world of the everyday. Slightly more fully, it means *a life of compassion and a passion for justice.* I need both of these words, "compassion" and "justice," for compassion without justice easily gets individualized or sentimentalized, and justice without compassion easily sounds like politics.

Compassion is utterly central to the teaching of Jesus. As those of you who have read one or more of my books on Jesus know, I see it as the core value, the ethical paradigm of the life of faithfulness to God as we see it in Jesus. Jesus sums up theology and ethics in a very short saying (six words in English). It is found in Luke 6:36 with a parallel in Matthew 5:48 (very early Q material for those of you who like to know things like that): "be compassionate as God is compassionate." The word for "compassionate" in both Hebrew and Aramaic is related to the word for "womb." Thus, to be compassionate is to be womblike, to be like a womb. God is womblike, Jesus says, therefore, you be womblike.

What does it mean to be womblike? Well, it means to be life-giving, nourishing. It means to feel what a mother feels for the children of her womb: tenderness, willing their well-being, finding her children precious and beautiful. It can also mean a fierceness, for a mother can be fierce when she sees the children of her womb being threatened or treated destructively. Compassion is not just a soft, cozy virtue. It can have passion and fierceness to it as well.

To speak of compassion as the core value of the Christian life may seem like old hat to us, like ho-hum. But contrasted for a moment to what some Christians have thought the Christian life is most centrally about, that it is really about righteousness—keeping your moral shirttails clean, avoiding being stained by the world—in that sense, the Christian life is profoundly different from compassion. In many ways, compassion is virtually the opposite of righteousness in that sense. Jesus, as a person, was filled with compassion, and he calls us to compassion.

Jesus was also filled with a passion for justice. This is probably the least understood part of the teaching of Jesus in the modern American church, and maybe throughout most of the church's history. It's because we often misunderstand what the word "justice" means or we understand it poorly. We sometimes think that justice has to do with punishment, with people getting what is coming to them for what they have done wrong. When we think that way, then we think that the opposite of justice is mercy. But in the Bible, the opposite of justice is not mercy; the opposite of justice is injustice.

Justice and injustice have to do with the way societies are structured, with the way political and economic systems are put together. Like the Hebrew social prophets before him, Jesus's passion for justice set him against the domination system of his world and time. It set him against a politically oppressive and economically exploitative system that had been designed by wealthy and powerful elites in their own narrow self-interests and then legitimated by religion. And the domination system of his time, like the domination systems of all time, had devastating effects on the lives of peasants.

Also, like the Hebrew social prophets, Jesus was a God-intoxicated voice of peasant socioreligious protest, and not just protest against the domination system, but also as an advocate of God's justice. God's justice is about social justice. God's justice is about the equitable distribution of God's earth, and a passion for God's justice sets you against all of those systems designed by people in their own narrow self-interests to benefit the few at the expense of the many.

Indeed, it was Jesus's passion for justice that got him killed. That is why the authorities, the powers that be, executed him. The journey of Lent reminds us of that too: that Jesus was killed; he didn't simply die.

In Luke 13, some Pharisees come to Jesus to warn him that Herod is planning to kill him. Jesus replies, "Go and tell that fox Herod"—"fox" in the world of the Jewish homeland in the first century did not mean a sly, cunning, wily creature; it had more the connotation of "skunk": "Go and tell that skunk Herod"—"that it is impossible for a prophet to be killed outside of Jerusalem." Then he speaks of Jerusalem: "Jerusalem, Jerusalem, the city that kills the prophets and stones those who are sent to it" (13:32–34).

It is Jerusalem, of course, not as the center of Judaism, but Jerusalem as the center of the native domination system, of that economically exploitative and politically oppressive system that radically impoverished peasants and drove them to an existence of destitution and desperation. Jesus is killed because of his passionate criticism of that system and his advocacy of the kingdom of God, which is what life would be like on earth if God were king and the domination systems of this world were not. This is the political meaning of Good Friday.

To connect this back to compassion, justice is the social form of compassion. Justice and compassion are not opposites or different things; justice is the social and political form of caring for the least of these. If we take Jesus seriously, we are called to both compassion and justice.

To move to my conclusion, following Jesus—the journey of Lent—means a radical centering in God in which our own well-being resides, reconnecting to a center of meaning and purpose and energy in our lives. It means a passion for compassion and justice in the world of the everyday. The gospel of Jesus is ultimately very simple. There is nothing complicated about this at all. The gospel invites us to stand with Jesus, to take Jesus seriously. Take seriously your relationship to God, and take seriously caring about what God cares about in the world.

Chapter 10

Renewing Our Image of Jesus

I HEAR VERY FEW SERMONS about Jesus. Perhaps this is because of the kinds of churches I have most frequently attended (Lutheran, Presbyterian, Episcopalian), though I think it is probably the same for most mainstream churches. True, sometimes a parable or saying or healing act of Jesus may be preached on, but I seldom hear a sermon about Jesus except at Christmas or in Holy Week (though not always then) and occasionally on other festivals that celebrate his divine identity.

Scarcely ever have I heard a sermon about what Jesus was like as a historical figure, or about his purpose as

Originally published in *The Christian Century,* August 28–September 4, 1985, pp. 764–67.

he saw it, or about the way he related to the society of his own time. If, as we affirm, the Word became flesh in Jesus, then surely the historical life of Jesus discloses something about that Word. Paul's recognition that "we no longer know Jesus according to the flesh" (2 Cor. 5:16) should not be construed to mean that Jesus's historical life is irrelevant.

I suspect this lack is because neither the popular image of Jesus nor the dominant scholarly image learned in seminary provides a gestalt of the historical Jesus suitable for mainstream preaching. The popular image—popular in the sense of most widely held—pictures Jesus's identity and purpose with great clarity: he was the only begotten Son of God, whose purpose was to die for the sins of the world. Christians and non-Christians alike share this image, drawn from the Gospels (especially John) and creeds, carried through the history of the West and nurtured by our culture's celebrations of Christmas and Easter. Christians are those who believe the image to be true, while non-Christians are those who do not.

The popular image of what Jesus was like continues to thrive in fundamentalist and much conservative preaching, but for those of us schooled in mainstream seminaries or divinity schools, that image died as part of our educational process. There, if not before, we learned that the popular image does not correspond to what Jesus was like as a figure of history. Rather, we saw that the popular portrait came about by projecting the church's later beliefs and images back into his ministry itself. We learned that in all likelihood Jesus did not speak as he does in John's Gospel; that even the synoptic Gospels are a complex mixture of historical memory and post-Easter interpretation; that the image of Jesus as one who deliberately gave his life for the sins of the world is the product of the church's sacrificial theology; and that Jesus probably did not proclaim his own exalted identity or even think of himself in such terms. In short, we came to see that the popular image was the product of Christian theology and Christian popular culture. The image of Jesus as one who proclaimed his identity in the most exalted terms known to Judaism, who asked his hearers to believe his claims, and whose purpose was to die for our sins itself died.

In part this conclusion resulted from the dominant scholarly understanding of Jesus that did emerge from the withering fire of historical criticism: that Jesus was the eschatological prophet who believed that the final judgment was coming in his generation. Originating with Bernhard Weiss and Albert Schweitzer around the turn of the century, this understanding (in a stripped-down version) was propounded by Rudolf Bultmann and his successors. Moreover, according to it, Jesus's conviction concerning the coming end was not simply an odd, adventitious belief he held, extraneous to some more important conviction, but was central to his sense of who he was and what his mission was. He himself was conscious of being "the eschatological prophet"; the crisis that runs throughout his teaching was the imminent end of the world; his historical purpose was to warn his hearers to repent before it was too late and to invite them to ground their existence in God, for the world was soon to pass away.

This view does yield some powerful existential insights that can readily be made the subject of Christian preaching. But as an image of the historical Jesus, it is very difficult to incorporate into the life of the church, for, according to it, Jesus was a mistaken preacher of the end; he was wrong about the most central conviction that animated his mission. It is difficult to imagine this tenet forming part of a sermon; I cannot recall a preacher ever saying, "This text tells us that Jesus expected the end of the world in his own time; he was wrong of course, but let's see what we can make of the text anyway." Indeed, I suspect that most pastors have held the dominant scholarly understanding at arm's length largely because of its unhelpfulness for Christian preaching and teaching. It is not only a speculative scholarly construction, but an unattractive image of what Jesus was like as a historical figure.

And so we in the mainstream churches believe we cannot know much about Jesus, and what we do know does not compel our imaginations. No wonder we are left with so faint an image.

Holy Man

First, *Jesus was vividly in touch with the world of Spirit.* Whatever else he was, he was a "holy man," to use a semi-technical term from the history of religions. The word "holy" here is not an adjective pointing to righteousness or purity, but is used in the sense made famous by Rudolf Otto: as a noun, pointing to the numinous, the *mysterium tremendum,* the awesome reality and power at the heart of existence. A holy man is a person who experiences the holy vividly and frequently, who is experientially in contact with the power of another realm, the power of the Spirit.

Such persons, known in many cultures and including both women and men, are delegates of the tribe to the other realm, to use an anthropological characterization. As such, they are mediators between the realm of the Spirit and this world, entering the former realm in order to mediate power from that world to this one, especially in deeds of healing. To state the two defining characteristics of such people as compactly as possible, they are mystics and healers.

Such figures are known not only worldwide, but specifically within the history of Israel. Moses and Elijah are the two great holy men of the Old Testament, both known for their direct encounters with the other world and for their deeds of power. The classical prophets of ancient Israel regularly report seeing into another world (see, e.g., the opening verse of Ezekiel: "The heavens were opened, and I saw visions of God"), though they are without the healing powers characteristic of the holy man proper. Contemporary with Jesus are several Jewish holy men, especially Honi the Circle-Drawer, Hanina ben Dosa, and, slightly later, St. Paul.

That Jesus belongs within this charismatic strand of Judaism is evident. According to the Gospel accounts, his ministry began with an experience of "the heavens opening" and the Spirit descending upon him; he applied to himself the words, "The Spirit of the Lord is upon me" (Luke 4:18); and he spoke of the Spirit as active through him. He practiced spiritual disciplines common to holy men: fasting, solitude, long hours of prayer (presumably contemplative), even an ordeal in the wilderness. He called God *Abba,* clearly reflective of an experiential intimacy with the holy. To his contemporaries, both friend and foe, he was known above all as a healer and exorcist, as one who mediated the power of the Spirit. Whatever else he was, he was a holy man.

Social Concern

There is a second feature of the historical Jesus that can significantly inform the life of the church today: his relationship to the society of his time. *He was deeply involved in the historical life of his own people.* Specifically, he saw them headed on a course toward historic catastrophe flowing out of their loyalties and blindness; he called his hearers to a radically different understanding of what faithfulness to God meant, an understanding that was to be embodied in the life of a community in history.

This connection to the life of his own time can be seen in his roles as prophet and renewal movement founder. As recent scholarship has emphasized, Jesus founded a renewal movement within Judaism that competed with other Jewish renewal movements for the allegiance of his contemporaries. Each had a different vision of what the people of God should be, each with different historical consequences. Jesus sharply denounced the path on which his people had embarked, including the ways advocated by the other renewal movements. He warned of catastrophic consequences—war, the destruction of Jerusalem and of the Temple—if their blindness continued.

Jesus's connection to the historical crisis of his time was obscured throughout much of this century by the portrait of him as the eschatological prophet. In that role, he was not seen to be concerned about historical matters. The crisis that he announced was the end of the world, not a historical crisis in the life of his people.

But almost without realizing it, recent scholarship has undermined the eschatological understanding of Jesus. That view was founded on the "coming Son of Man" sayings (e.g., Mark 13:24–27) as authentic to Jesus; yet New Testament scholars now routinely (and, I think, correctly) deny that the "coming Son of Man" sayings go back to Jesus. For the most part, however, the undermining goes unnoticed; the portrait of Jesus as eschatological prophet remains, despite the disappearance of its foundation.

But if the crisis that Jesus announced was not the imminent end of the world, what was it? It was a coming historical catastrophe, probably not yet inevitable, that would result from the combination of Rome's imperial needs and insensitivity to the cultural direction of his own people. Like an Old Testament prophet (to whom he was compared by his contemporaries), Jesus criticized the present path and threatened destruction if it did not change.

As a prophet and renewal movement founder, Jesus called his hearers into "an alternative community with an alternative consciousness," to use Old Testament scholar Walter Brueggemann's illuminating phrase.[1] The marks of his renewal movement stand out sharply against the background of his time. His acceptance of the outcasts—one of his most radical acts—pointed to an identity defined by one's relationship to God rather than by cultural standards of performance. He proclaimed the way of peace instead of war, both in his teaching and in the deliberately dramatic manner in which he entered Jerusalem on an animal that symbolized peace rather than war, an action very much in the tradition of prophetic acts in the Old Testament. The Jesus movement was the "peace party" within Judaism, as Gerd Theissen puts it.[2]

In place of "holiness" as the *imitatio dei* followed by the other renewal movements ("You shall be holy, for I the LORD your God am holy," Lev. 19:2), Jesus substituted a different blueprint for the life of the community: "Be compassionate as your heavenly father is compassionate" (Luke 6:36). Moreover, this directive was intended for the earthly life of the people of God. Jesus's intention was the transformation of his people in the face of a historical crisis.

These are potent themes for our own times. They invite us to take very seriously the two central presuppositions of the Jewish-Christian tradition. First, there is a dimension or realm of reality beyond (and beneath) the visible world of our ordinary experience, a dimension charged with power whose ultimate quality is compassion. Second, the fruits of a life lived in accord with the Spirit are to be embodied not only in individuals, but also in the life of the faithful community. In short, God cares about the shape and texture of historical communities—and sometimes "hands them over" to the consequences of their own blindness.

Yet these themes are also threatening to us. The first threatens our sense of normalcy. What if it is true, as Huston Smith argues, that the world of our ordinary experience is but one level of reality and that we are at all times surrounded by other dimensions of reality that we commonly do not experience?[3] Such a view challenges the practical atheism of much of our culture and church. The claim that there really is a realm of Spirit is both exciting and oddly disconcerting.

The second theme threatens our comfort within contemporary culture. The historical Jesus, with his call to a countercommunity with a counterconsciousness (including consciousness of another realm), challenges the central values of contemporary American culture. Increasingly, our understanding of reality is one-dimensional, even within the church; our quest for fulfillment seeks satisfaction through greater consumption; our security rests in nuclear weapons; and our blindness and idolatry are visible in our stated willingness to blow up the world, if need be, to preserve our way of life. We are called to become the church in a culture whose values are largely alien to the Christian message, to be once again the church of the catacombs.

Images of Jesus give content to what loyalty to him means. The popular picture of Jesus as one whose purpose was to proclaim truths about himself most often construes loyalty to him as insistence on the truth of those claims. Loyalty becomes belief in the historical truthfulness of all the statements in the Gospels. The absence of an image—the most common fruit of mainstream theological education—leaves us with no clear notion of what it means to take Jesus seriously, no notion of what loyalty might entail, no rudder for the life of discipleship. But the image of Jesus as a man of Spirit, deeply involved in the historical crisis of his own time, besides being more historically adequate than either the popular or the dominant scholarly image, can shape the church's discipleship today.

Chapter 11

Healing Our Image of God

Today I want to talk about the character of God, about how we see the character of God and the effects of this on the Christian life. Or to turn it into a question, "What Is the Character of Your God?"

I want to explain a bit more about what I mean when I speak about the character of God. The character of God has to do with the very nature of God. It is deeper than the will of God, for will flows out of character. So my question is: What is God's character? What does God care about? What is God's passion? Our sense of God's character, our

Sermon delivered at Calvary Episcopal Church, Memphis, Tennessee, as part of the Lenten Noonday Preaching Series, March 24, 2000.

perception of what God is like, is conveyed by our images of or metaphors for God. I typically distinguish between concepts of God, which I see as more abstract, and images of God—images or metaphors are more concrete, more visual. Indeed, I sometimes think of metaphors as linguistic art or verbal art. Some of the biblical metaphors or images for God include the following: God is like a king, like a judge, like a shepherd, like a father and, less commonly, like a mother. God is like a lover, like a potter, like a warrior, and so forth.

These images for God matter, to repeat my foundational claim. They matter because they shape how we see the character of God. I want to talk about two primary images or metaphors for God's character that have dominated the Jewish and Christian traditions throughout their long history, reaching back into biblical times. They are two very different models for the character of God. A model, as Sallie McFague, an author and theologian from Vanderbilt Divinity School, puts it, is a metaphor with "staying power." To which I would add, a model is a way of constellating or gestalting metaphors. That is, the biblical metaphors for God gravitate toward one or the other of these two models or primary images for God. Both of these have been present throughout Christian history. Both are alive in the contemporary church. But they are so different from each other that they virtually produce two different religions, both using the same language.

The first of these models or ways of imaging God's character sees God as the lawgiver and judge who also loves us. This is the one that I grew up with and the one I suspect that many of you grew up with. It is probably also the most common or visible image of God within the Christian church today. As lawgiver, God gave us the Ten Commandments and other laws about how to live. God told us what is expected of us.

As judge, God was also the enforcer of the law; there would be a judgment someday. (I took all of this very much for granted when I was growing up in the church.) And God also loved us. Because we weren't very good at being good, we weren't very good at keeping God's laws, God provided an alternate means of satisfying God's law—of becoming right with God. In Old Testament times this was accomplished through Temple sacrifice as a way of atoning for disobedience. In New Testament times, God sent Jesus to be the sacrifice, to die for our sins, thus making our forgiveness possible.

God did love us, but it was a conditional love. Namely, God would accept us if—and here again you can fill in the blank—if we were good enough, if our repentance was earnest enough, if we believed in Jesus. So, even though God loved us, the system of requirements remained. God as lawgiver and judge in a way triumphs over the love of God. The dynamic of sin, guilt, and forgiveness and doing or believing what we needed to were the central components of the Christian life.

It is striking to me how pervasive this dynamic of sin, guilt, and forgiveness is in even liberal Christian settings. A couple summers ago, I was at a weeklong event in a classically liberal Christian institution. Each day began with a chapel service at nine o'clock in the morning attended by several hundred people, and every day that chapel service began with a confession of sin. I thought to myself, "Dear Lord. It's nine o'clock in the morning, and we've already been bad."

Now, I have no illusions about our being perfect or anything like that. I'm just commenting that this dynamic of sin, guilt, and forgiveness is directly correlated with imaging God as the lawgiver and judge who also loves us. I have since learned to call this model of God the *monarchical model* of God, from the word "monarch," or king. I owe that phrase to the theologians Ian Barbour and Sallie McFague. This monarchical model of God takes its name from the common biblical metaphor of God as lord and king.

As king, God is both lawgiver and judge, and we don't measure up very well in our relationship to God as lawgiver and judge. Who are we in relationship to God as shepherd? We are sheep, of course. Who are we in relationship to God as lawgiver and judge? Well, we're a defendant. We're on trial, as it were, and this life, the life we have right now, is about getting it right or doing what we need to do. Depending upon the particular form of Christianity with which we grew up, getting it right might be some combination of right behavior or right belief, with the mixture put together in various ways.

This model is softened somewhat, but not much, when parental imagery is substituted for king imagery. Of course, it's usually father imagery that gets substituted for king imagery. But when the monarchical God is imaged as a parent rather than as a king, it is as the critical parent. It's God as the disappointed parent, the parent who loves us, yes, but who on the whole isn't all that pleased with how we've turned out. The monarchical model is thus God as the divine superego in our heads. That voice that ranges along a spectrum from "You're no good" to "You're never quite enough."

This way of imaging God's character, this model, has several effects on the Christian life. I will very briefly mention four. As I mention them, ask yourself if you have known forms of Christianity like this. The first of these is that the monarchical God is the God of requirements. It suggests that the Christian life is about measuring up, of doing or believing what God requires of us.

Second, this way of imaging God's character leads to an in-group and out-group distinction. There are those who measure up and those who don't. There are those who are saved and those who are not.

Third, ultimately the monarchical model of God is a God of vengeance. It's a strong statement, but think about it for a moment. In this way of thinking about God, God is going to get all of those people who do not measure up, who do not meet the requirements. There will be a judgment, either after death with the prospect of heaven or hell or at the second coming.

To cite a memorable and provocative phrase from my colleague John Dominic Crossan: the most common Christian vision of the second coming is as "divine ethnic cleansing." Of course, those who hold to this model would never speak of it that way. But think of those visions of the second coming that basically amount to "God is going to get all of those people who are not like us."

Finally, fourth, rather than liberating us from self-preoccupation, this is the God who focuses our attention on our own salvation, on making sure that we have done or believed what we're supposed to.

There is another image of God, another primary model for imaging God's character in the biblical tradition as well as in the postbiblical Christian tradition. To give it a short-hand label, I call this one the *divine-lover model*. The image of God as lover is very interesting when you think about it; and it's deeply rooted in the biblical tradition. It occurs frequently in the prophets of the Hebrew Bible. To cite just one example from the prophets, from Isaiah 43, that wonderful chapter of gospel in the Hebrew Bible, God is portrayed as saying to Israel, "You are precious in my sight, and honored, and I love you. . . . Do not fear" (43:4–5).

The image of God as lover is the central image in the Song of Solomon, that collection of erotic love poetry also known as the Song of Songs. By the way, a phrase like Song of Songs or Holy of Holies is the Hebrew way of phrasing a superlative. The Holy of Holies is the holiest place. The Song of Songs is the best song, understood by Jews and Christians alike through the centuries as an allegory of divine love. It is striking that the Song of Songs was the single most popular biblical book among Christians of the Middle Ages. More manuscript copies of that book survived than of any other book in the Bible.

The image of God as lover is also widespread in the New Testament. It is found in the best-known verse, John 3:16, which as you all know begins, "For God so loved the world . . ." God is seen as lover, and Jesus is the embodiment, the incarnation of the love of God. To image God as lover changes the dynamic of the Christian life dramatically. God is "in love" with us. We are precious in God's sight and honored. We are the beloved of God. That's who we are in relationship to God as lover. God yearns for us.

As the author and theologian Roberta Bondi, from Candler School of Theology at Emory University in Atlanta, puts it in one of her books, "God is besotted with us." That single five-word sentence stood out in neon lights for me when I first read it. "God is besotted with us." For just a moment think how your life would be different if you knew, at the deepest level of your being, that God is besotted with you, that God yearns for you, yearns that you turn and be in relationship with God as the beloved of God.

It's very different from the monarchical model. The monarchical model puts us on guard. There are requirements to be met, rewards and punishments to be considered. We are defendants on trial. But the divine-lover model changes the way we see the character of God. Rather than being the one we need to please, whether through good deeds or earnest repentance and faith, God as lover is passionate about us, yearns to be in relationship with us. Yet there is a danger to the divine-lover model. The danger is that it can become too individualistic, too sweet, as it were, as if the focus was primarily on *me*. We need to guard against sentimentalizing and individualizing this image, for the image of God as lover means that God loves everybody, not just me and not just us, but everybody.

So the image of God as lover is very much associated with a concreteness and particularity of life in this world. As lover, God is liberating. This is the central theme of the most important story that ancient Israel knew, the story of the exodus from Egypt, which meant liberation from an oppression that was simultaneously economic, political, and religious. Images of God as liberator continue through Israel's history and into the New Testament. It is not God's will that we be slaves in bondage, whether internally or externally.

As lover, God is compassionate. This is God's character. Compassion, as many of you know, is an unusually rich metaphor in the Bible. It's related to the word for "womb." To say that God is compassionate is to say that God is like a womb or "womblike," life-giving, nourishing. Compassion in the Bible also has resonances associated with the feelings that a mother has for the children of her womb. What are the feelings that a mother has for the children of her womb? Tenderness, of course. She wills their well-being and is filled with hope and concern.

And feelings from the womb aren't simply soft. They can become fierce, as when the children of a mother's womb are threatened or badly treated. Just as a mother feels compassion for her children, wills their well-being, and can become fierce in the defense of them, so God feels compassion for us as God's children, wills our well-being, and can become fierce in defense of us all.

As lover, God is not only compassionate, but also passionate about social justice. God as lover is passionate about social justice with a simple reason that its opposite, systemic injustice, is the single greatest source of unnecessary human social misery, of unnecessary human suffering in history. Social justice is the way our well-being is attained in this world. Indeed, God as lover is "in love" not only with us as human beings, but even with the nonhuman world, with the whole of creation. Thus both a passion for justice and a passion for the environment flow out of imaging God as lover.

Depending upon which of these ways of imaging God's character is emphasized, the character of God is seen very differently, and the Christian life is seen very differently. Is it about meeting requirements so that we might be saved someday, or is it about a relationship in the here and now with God as lover? The ethical imperative that goes with each is quite different. For the monarchical model the ethical imperative is, "Be good, because you will be called to account. There will be a judgment." For the divine-lover model the ethical imperative is, "Love what God loves." So what is the character of your God?

One of the most wonderful postbiblical expressions of God as the divine lover is from George Herbert's poem

"Love Bade Me Welcome," which some of you will recognize. Herbert was a seventeenth-century Anglican poet, one of the great Anglican lyrical spiritual poets. I want to close by reading this relatively short poem to you, "Love Bade Me Welcome." The poem is set up as a dialogue. One partner is Love, which is Herbert's word for God, so when you hear the word "Love" here, you might think "God." The other partner in the dialogue is an imaginary person, perhaps Herbert himself.

> Love bade me welcome, yet my soul drew back,
>   Guilty of dust and sin.
> But quick-ey'd Love, observing me grow slack
>   From my first entrance in,
> Drew nearer to me, sweetly questioning
>   If I lack'd anything.
>
> "A guest," I answer'd "worthy to be here";
>   Love said, "You shall be he."
> "I, the unkind, the ungrateful? Ah, my dear,
>   I cannot look on thee."
> Love took my hand, and smiling did reply,
>   "Who made the eyes but I?"
>
> "Truth, Lord, but I have marr'd them; let my shame
>   Go where it doth deserve."
> "And know you not," says Love "who bore the blame?"
>   "My dear, then I will serve."

"You must sit down," says Love "and taste my meat."
  So I did sit and eat.

There are many ways of thinking about the Lenten journey of death and resurrection. Today I want to suggest that one of its meanings is dying to life under the lawgiver and judge and rising to new life as the beloved of God.

Life is short, and we do not have too much time to gladden the hearts of those who travel the way with us. So be swift to love, and make haste to be kind. And the blessings of God, Creator, Christ, and ever-present Spirit go with you this day and forever more.

Chapter 12

Living God's Passion

IT'S SO GOOD TO SEE SO MANY of you gathered together under the umbrella Progressive Christians Uniting. You are one of the very encouraging signs of our times, as I think you all know there is a major change under way in mainline denominations in this country today, and also in the progressive wing of evangelical churches as well as a growing political consciousness. There is also a growing recovery of the riches of our tradition, when we understand that tradition nonliterally and nonexclusively.

We will be talking about progressive Christianity, or what I sometimes call emerging Christianity, or even for

Keynote speech to Progressive Christians Uniting, Pasadena, California, February 19, 2007.

the sake of claiming our deep roots neo-traditional Christianity. I don't expect that last term to catch on. But I am not willing to let our more conservative brothers and sisters have the word "traditional." There is so much about the Christian right that is modern and has no roots in the Christian past at all, even for many Christians who would speak of themselves as orthodox rather than as part of the Christian right. So much of what passes for orthodoxy today is really the product of the conflict between the Enlightenment and Christianity and the hardening of notions like infallibility and inherency, which were not part of the premodern Christian past at all.

The major feature that I am going to talk about tonight is the growing awareness among progressive Christians of the political dimensions of the Bible and of Jesus. Indeed, "dimension" is too weak a term for what I am going to talk about, for it's not just *that* the Bible has a political dimension; in fact, it is one of two focal points of the Bible, one of two focal points of what it means to follow Jesus. These two focal points are two transformations. One of them is personal transformation; the other one is social transformation. Though I am going to talk primarily about social and political transformation tonight, it's important for those of us who have become passionate about social transformation not to neglect the personal dimension of the Christian gospel. The Christian life is about a deepening centering in God, *and* it is about social transformation.

I am using "social transformation" in its broadest meaning, the transformation of the world, the humanly created world of culture, the world of systems, political systems, economic systems, and systems of convention. As I thought about what I might say to you tonight, I realized that in many ways I am speaking to the choir. We are already, I think, all on the same page about this. So I decided not to try to tell you something you don't know or to try to persuade you of something. Instead, I am defining my task as: How do we help other Christians to see the political passion of our own tradition? How do we do consciousness raising about this in our local communities, our local congregations?

Here I want to stress what an enormous resource the network of local congregations throughout this country is. I sometimes have said that Christianity has more outlets than Coca-Cola does. I am not sure that's completely correct, but for those of us who are Christians, we have a network in place, and our audience is to a large extent the communities that we are part of. My perception of mainline Christians today is that maybe 60 or 70 percent are pretty committed to a political stance. But there is still a significant percentage who are apolitical or who could go either way. If we could change the voting patterns of, say, 20 or 10 percent of mainline Christians in that center bloc, it would change the makeup of state legislatures in most states, and it would change the makeup of national politics as well.

How do we help people to see the political passion of the Bible? It's often been overlooked throughout all the centuries of Christianity's domestication by the dominant culture. I am going to talk about "God's Passion and Ours," and part two will be the subtitle, "Mysticism and Empowerment, Resistance and Advocacy."

God's Passion and Ours

I suggest that in our local religious communities we educate people about God's passion and invite them to reflect on it. I am using the word "passion" here not primarily in the sense of suffering, though I think it makes sense to speak of the suffering of God. I am using "passion" in the sense that we use the word when we ask somebody, "What are you passionate about? What's the passion of your life?" My suggestion is that we ask, "What is God's passion? What is God passionate about? What is God's dream for the earth?"

For Christians, the answer to that question is that we see God's passion in the *Bible* and *Jesus*. They are our two primary ways of knowing about the character and passion of God. So my suggestion is that we help people to see the passion of God initially in the Jewish Bible, the Christian Old Testament. The key to suddenly making the political focus of the Jewish Bible clear is showing people the world of the Bible. Now, I and many others have written about this in many places, so I am going to describe the *social world of the Bible* with four short phrases.

It was *politically oppressive;* that is, the ancient world was ruled by monarchs, aristocracies, and so forth. Most premodern societies from the invention and growth of large-scale agriculture, so from about 3000 BCE, onward, were *economically exploitative.* The wealthiest 1 to 2 percent of the population typically acquired half to two-thirds of the wealth in these societies. These were preindustrial societies, so that wealth came from agricultural production. The powerful elites set the system up in such a way that wealth from agriculture flowed into their coffers. Third, power in these societies was *legitimated by religion.* It was commonly said that the king ruled by divine right. The monarch or the emperor would frequently be called the "son of God." The social order was said to reflect the will of God. Humans didn't create it; God set it up this way. Fourth and finally, these societies were *chronically violent.* I am not speaking so much here about criminal violence. I am talking about war. Wars in the premodern world were initiated primarily by the powerful and wealthy elites for the sake of increasing the amount of agricultural production they controlled, for that was the only way they could increase their wealth. The term for this very common way of organizing the world is the ancient, or premodern, *domination system.*

Once one realizes that this is the world of the Jewish Bible as well as of the Christian Testament, then it becomes almost transparently clear what the God of the Bible is passionate about. Let me illustrate that very quickly with the two main portions of the Jewish Bible, the Law and the Prophets. Of course there is the third, the Writings, but the Law and the Prophets were sacred scripture by the time of Jesus. The Law is the Torah (the Pentateuch), the first five books of the Bible. At the center of the Torah is ancient Israel's story of the exodus. You all know this, but we need to help people understand the significance of this. The story of the exodus is what the Old Testament scholar Walter Brueggemann calls Israel's primal narrative—its originating narrative—and also its most important story. And what is that story about? It's about liberation from economic and political bondage and the creation of an alternative community marked by no monarchy, no elites, and a passion for economic justice as evidenced in the rules about land, among other things.

The second main portion of the Jewish Bible, the Prophets, speaks very concisely about the rise, failure, and fall of the monarchy. The prophets were voices of God-intoxicated socioreligious protest against the injustice and wars of the monarchy. The two central concerns of the prophets, what they say is the dream of God, are justice and peace. Here it's important to try to raise consciousness about this by clarifying what is meant by the word "justice," because a lot of Americans think of justice primarily as punitive or criminal justice. The central justice issue in the Bible is economic justice.

The Bible doesn't know about racism, partly because racism was not an issue in the ancient world. The Bible doesn't know about democracy. The Bible doesn't know about sexism; generally speaking, it legitimates patriarchy. The central justice issue is economic justice, or distributive justice: that everybody should have enough, not as a function of charity but as the product of justice. That's the central indictment that the prophets direct against the native domination system in their time. That system served the cause of injustice, which is about the abuse and exploitation of the poor, who were roughly 90 percent of the population.

We find these two concerns, justice and peace, brought together in a marvelous passage in Micah. You know the first part of the passage best from Isaiah 2:2–4, but the same passage in Micah 4 has some additional lines. The part that is very familiar to everybody is the dream of God as a time when the nations "shall beat their swords into plowshares, and their spears into pruning hooks; neither shall they learn war any more" (4:3).

Then at the very end of that passage Micah adds: "They shall all sit under their own vines and under their own fig trees" (4:4). It's an image of everybody having their own land and sitting under their own vines, their own fig trees. This isn't about subsistence; this isn't about a meager amount of bread. This is about vines and fig trees. I was in my early thirties when I had my first fresh fig. I didn't know anything like that grew on trees—they are magnificent, sweet, delicious. I mean, this is gourmet food we are talking about here. My point is, God's dream for a world of peace is a world in which everybody has what they need for a good life. Then the last phrase of the Micah passage: "And no one shall make them afraid" (4:4). I can't resist the footnote that we live in a culture that plays the fear card again and again and again.

So what's the dream of God according to the Jewish Bible? Very simply, a world of compassion, justice, and peace. Compassion and justice, I want to underline, are intrinsically related. Justice is the social form of compassion, and compassion is the heart of justice. This is a political vision. More precisely, it's a theopolitical vision—not theocratic, but theopolitical. It's about politics in the most important sense of the word, about the shaping of society, the shaping of the social world in which we live. This theopolitical vision continues in Jesus in early Christianity, and so I turn to the second half of part one.

The passion of God is revealed in *Jesus*. My springboard here is that for Christians Jesus is the decisive revelation or disclosure of what can be seen of God in a human life. So for Christians Jesus is the decisive revelation of the passion of God. What was Jesus's passion? It's twofold: God and the kingdom of God. When I say his passion was God, I mean he grew up in a God-saturated tradition. I think it's a sound historical judgment to say that Jesus was a Jewish mystic, and mystics always become passionate about God. Jesus's message was both an invitation and an imperative to practice a way that was radically centered in God.

The other passion of Jesus's life is closely related to that, the kingdom of God. When helping people to see what this is about, remind them that the kingdom is "Your kingdom come on earth as it is in heaven," and to quote my colleague Dom Crossan, one of his great one-liners: "Heaven's in great shape. Earth is where the problems are." The kingdom of God is for the earth; the idea that the kingdom of God is about an afterlife is a very unfortunate notion. There is no denial of an afterlife here, but that's not what the kingdom of God is about.

The phrase "kingdom of God" is both a political and religious metaphor in the first-century world. Religious: it is the kingdom of God. Political: the heirs of Jesus lived under other kingdoms. A "kingdom" was the most common form of political and social organization. People knew about the kingdom of Herod, they knew about the kingdom of Rome. Rome did not refer to itself as an empire, but as a kingdom. When people heard Jesus talking about the kingdom of God, they knew it must have been something different from the kingdom of Herod or the kingdom of Rome. Put very simply, the kingdom of God is what life would be like on earth if God were king and the rulers of the domination systems of this world were not.

And, of course, "kingdom of God" is the most central phrase in all of Jesus's teaching. All New Testament scholars agree about this. Just to cite one verse, "Strive first for the kingdom of God and God's justice" (Matt. 6:33). That's normally translated "righteousness"—"Strive first for the kingdom of God and God's righteousness"—but it's really important to realize that most often in the Bible the word "righteousness" means "justice." It doesn't mean some kind of individual rectitude that "makes a man so damn righteous he's no earthly good." I think that's a line from Will Rogers. In modern English "righteousness" commonly refers to personal virtue of a particularly rigorous kind. In the Bible it almost always means justice.

"Strive first for the kingdom of God and God's justice, and all these things will be given to you as well."

We're still talking about how we help people to see this with the figure of Jesus. Two days from now is Ash Wednesday and the beginning of Lent, which climaxes in Holy Week. Lent and Holy Week offer an extraordinary opportunity for raising consciousness about the political meaning of Jesus. It sounds as though I am selling a book that John Dominic Crossan and I coauthored, *The Last Week*. What we do in that book is a day-by-day account of the last week of Jesus's life as told in the Gospel of Mark. We are not speculating about what's behind this. We are just saying, look at the text.

That week begins with an anti-imperial entry into Jerusalem. We all know the Palm Sunday story, in which Jesus rides into Jerusalem on a donkey. What few people realize is that that way of entry into the city symbolized a king of peace who would banish the warhorse and the battle bowl from the land. And even fewer people know that on that same day, from the other side of the city, the Roman governor, Pilate, rode at the head of a large number of imperial troops and cavalry coming up to Jerusalem to reinforce the imperial garrison on the Temple Mount for the week of Passover, which was often a time of disturbance. It's real clear just reading Mark that Jesus planned his entrance in advance. This was a planned political counterdemonstration.

That's Sunday. The anti-imperial entry of Sunday is followed on Monday by the anti–Temple authorities action.

The overturning of the tables of the money changers was again clearly planned in advance. This is not what some people have cheaply called the "Temple Tantrum," as if Jesus saw what was going on, got really mad, and just did it in a fit of anger. It was planned in advance. And that's a symbolic act, like the ones the great prophets of the Jewish Bible would sometimes perform. They would perform an action to symbolize something and gather a crowd, and then they would speak about it. What Jesus says after the tables of the money changers have been overturned begins with a quotation from Isaiah in which God says: "My house shall be called a house of prayer for all the nations" (56:7). Then comes the indictment: "But you have made it a den of robbers," a quotation from Jeremiah 7:11. It's clear in Jeremiah that the people who have made the Temple a den of robbers are the Temple authorities, the wealthy and powerful elites who have ignored justice. By quoting that passage Jesus is indicting the contemporary Temple authorities, who have colluded with Roman imperial authority in the administration of the domination systems in the Jewish homeland in the first century.

Holy Week is full of political passion. I am not going to take you through Tuesday, Wednesday, and Thursday, but go to Friday. Jesus was executed by established authority. Christians live in the only major religious tradition whose founder was executed by established authority. We ought to be taken aback by that. Of course if you want to extend it, it's not just Jesus. Paul, the second most important person in the formation of early Christianity, was executed by imperial authority. Peter, the third most important person, was executed by imperial authority. If you think James was the fourth most important person, he also was executed by the authorities. What is this, a string of bad luck? There was something that the authorities quite frankly did not care for in Jesus's proclamation of the kingdom of God and the following that gathered around him because of it.

Now, I am utterly convinced Jesus was nonviolent. But it was about resistance nonetheless, and this involved a radical critique of the powers that ruled his world. So Good Friday has a profound political meaning. And then plug in Easter. Now, Easter has many nuances of meaning. But within this framework, if Good Friday is the powers that be saying no to Jesus, then Easter is God's yes to Jesus and to the passion of Jesus. Easter is God's vindication of Jesus. Of course it's more than that, but it's inescapable that it is that. In Peter's address to the authorities in the book of Acts, he says, "Therefore let the entire house of Israel know with certainty that God has made him both Lord and Messiah, this Jesus whom you crucified" (2:36). A simple summary: for Christians, God's passion is that we center in God as known in the Bible and Jesus, that we be compassionate, and that we seek justice.

Mysticism and Empowerment, Resistance and Advocacy

I turn now to part two, which leads to my conclusion. Part two is based on four words: "Mysticism and Empowerment,

Resistance and Advocacy." My claim in this section is very simple; namely, it is important that we have a spiritual center, a grounding, a base that empowers us to resist the forces that create injustice and violence and to advocate for alternatives.

I owe two of these terms to the subtitle of an important book by the theologian Dorothee Soelle, who died in April 2003. It's a book I really commend to you. The main title is *The Silent Cry*. The subtitle is *Mysticism and Resistance*. The central claim in this book is that mysticism, far from being otherworldly or escapist, has often been the source of Christian political resistance throughout the centuries. It's interesting to reflect on the great reformers, and not just the Protestant Reformers, but monastic and other reformers in the history of Christianity. I think they all were mystics or certainly had mystical experiences. That was really what gave them the impetus for what they were doing.

To her two words "mysticism" and "resistance" I have added "empowerment" and "advocacy." These may be implicit in her title, but I think it's important to make them explicit. So let me now very briefly say something about each of those words.

I use the term *mysticism* in its broadest sense, and I want very quickly to name two kinds of mysticism. One is ecstatic mysticism, by which I mean the vivid experience of God or the sacred that involves a nonordinary state of consciousness that makes ordinary consciousness seem like sleep or a kind of blindness and makes God utterly real for those who have such an experience. Then there is what I am going to call nonecstatic mysticism. Now, I haven't really thought very much about this kind before, but I am very much aware that Gandhi could be spoken of as a mystic, even though I am not aware that he spoke of having any ecstatic experiences. Nonecstatic mysticism I would define as union with the will of God, ecstatic mysticism as communion with the sacred. What these two forms of mysticism have in common is a deep centering in God.

And that leads to the second term, *empowerment.* Centering in God empowers. It's a source of courage. It gives you a place to stand. It is the source of what philosopher and theologian Paul Tillich called the "courage to be": the courage to stand against the powers, to stand even when steeples are falling. Mysticism and empowerment most often or at least very often lead to *resistance,* the third term, resistance to the way things are, because you have come to know that things can be different and that the powers that rule this world are not the ultimate powers. And then the fourth term, *advocacy.* It's not just about standing against; it's about standing for. It is about both.

If we only stand for without standing against, we risk becoming banal. Most people want the world to be a better place. But if we don't take seriously a critical discernment of and name what is wrong, our desire for a better world risks becoming a cliché. So yes, it's both a standing for *and* a standing against. Does this mean we are to stand against domination systems, domestic, national, and international? Of course. It means that we are to stand for an alternative vision of what life on earth can be like. Does this mean that we, as American Christians, are to stand against American imperial behavior? Of course. This involves minimally a renunciation of the right to preemptive war and a deep commitment to multilateralism, for the only way an empire can control its intrinsic tendency toward hubris is to relate to the other nations of the world as if they are peers and take their perspectives very, very seriously. We all know that if an individual has narcissistic tendencies, the only real cure for that is for that person's judgment to be subject to the critical reflection of others. Empires are intrinsically narcissistic.

Does this mean we will stand against the exploitation and degradation of the environment? Of course, for nature, the nonhuman world, matters not just for our future; it matters to God. Here one of the most familiar passages in the whole of the Christian Bible says it so simply: "For God so loved the world" (John 3:16). Not just you and me and us, not just Christians, not just people, but God so loved the world. The world matters to God. "The earth is the Lord's and all that is in it" (Ps. 24:1). It is not there for us to divide up, so that some people get a lot of it and other people get none of it, and it's not there for us as a species to use as we wish.

To bring this to a close, ultimately it seems to me the Christian message is simple. We have sometimes made it so complex with our tendency toward overprecision in matters of doctrine, attempts at great clarity, and all of that. It's so simple. Ground yourself in God, center in God. It is the way of life. It is the way of empowerment. Participate in God's passion, participate in God's dream. Love the world as God loves the world, and change the world.

Chapter 13

Facing Today's Challenges

AN INTERVIEW

M Y NAME IS MARCUS BORG. I am probably best known
as an author of books on the Bible and Jesus and God
or generally, I suppose, religion. I taught for many years at
Oregon State University, where I held the Hundere Chair
of Religion and Culture. I retired from that about a year
ago, and I'm now Canon Theologian at Trinity Episcopal Cathedral in Portland, Oregon. Most of my time these
days is spent traveling—mostly in the United States—
and speaking to church groups. I travel about a hundred

Originally published on *ExploreFaith.org,* June 2009.

thousand miles a year. The other thing that I do professionally, vocationally, is to write books. My most recent book just published, right around March 1, is *The First Paul,* coauthored with John Dominic Crossan. It's a book that separates the genuine letters of Paul—the seven all scholars agree were written by him—from the six letters that are probably not written by him. The title, *The First Paul,* refers to the Paul of the seven genuine letters, and he's an incredibly attractive figure, as radical in his own right as the figure of Jesus is. Dom Crossan and I think that's an important case to make, because many people who like Jesus find Paul to be a real turnoff. In fact, the opening chapter of our book is called "Paul: An Appealing or Appalling Apostle?" And then, in addition to that, my first novel has been accepted, and it'll be published in about a year, early winter of 2010. The title is *Putting Away Childish Things.*[1] I've never written fiction before, so maybe this is a new chapter in my life.

The past few years have seen numerous bestsellers from a group of writers known as the New Atheists. These writers claim that there is no proof that God exists and that belief is naive, delusional, and has resulted in great evil. What is your response to these charges?

I think the best known of the books on atheism that have made the *New York Times* bestseller list are Sam Harris's *The End of Faith,* Christopher Hitchens's *God Is Not Great,* and Richard Dawkins's *The God Delusion.* What these books share in common is that they attack the most common understanding of the word "God," at least in Western culture, namely, that the word "God" refers to a personlike being, a superpowerful authority figure separate from the universe who created the universe a long time ago and, from time to time, intervenes.

In shorthand, I call that way of thinking about God "supernatural theism." And I think they're right about that "God." I don't believe in that understanding of God either. However, their books basically ignore another understanding of what the word "God" means that goes way back to antiquity. It's found in the most ancient forms of the religions of the world—so does the other understanding of God, by the way; they run side by side throughout the history of the religions.

This other understanding of God does not think of God as a personlike being separate from the universe, but, rather, understands that the word "God" refers to a, for want of a better word, a "spiritual reality that interpenetrates the universe." That God is the encompassing spirit, if you will, in whom everything that is lives. I think the most compact biblical expression of that is found in Acts 17:28, in words attributed to Paul, that God is the one "in whom we live and move and have our being." Notice how the language works: we are in God, we live within God, we have our being within God, so that God is this encompassing spirit in whom everything that is lives.

To give you a postbiblical expression of this, the early Christian theologian Irenaeus, writing around the year 200, said this: "God contains everything, and nothing

179

contains God." Again, it's the same image: everything is in God, and yet God is more than the sum total of everything. That understanding of God has a technical name: it's called panentheism. All three parts of that word are important: it means that everything is in God.

These three writers, the New Atheists, if you will, seem to know nothing about that other understanding of God. Or when they do occasionally mention it, they dismiss it almost immediately as playing with words, not understanding that this is a very ancient understanding of God, probably most directly associated with the mystics and mysticism.

So when somebody says, "Well, I don't really believe in God" or "Those New Atheists, they really make a good case for there not being a God," my response always is, "Tell me about the God you don't believe in" and almost always it's the God of supernatural theism.

There is truth in these books by the New Atheists, but I think it's a limited truth. The truth that is in those books is that a very common understanding of God makes no compelling, persuasive sense. This is that understanding of God as the "Big Eye in the Sky" that sees everything we do and keeps kind of moral track of us. This is the God who sometimes intervenes to help people, but not consistently. This is the God in whose name the most horrible things have been done. God has been used to legitimate perhaps the most brutal activities that human beings have engaged in. So these writers correctly point out that religion—and let me use the plural, religions—as historical phenomena are profoundly ambiguous. Some of the greatest evil in the history of the world has been done in the name of religion.

At the same time, the religions have produced some of the greatest saints and greatest human beings who have ever lived. So there's a half-truth in these books and that half-truth is: every religion has much to be ashamed of. But it's only a partial truth.

What does Jesus teach us about prayer?

We know from the Gospels that Jesus practiced a form of contemplative prayer. We're not told exactly what kind, but we know that there was contemplative prayer in the Jewish tradition.

Contemplative prayer, of course, is the prayer of internal silence; we seek to sit silently in the presence of God and oftentimes experience ourselves descending to a deep level of the self, where we open out into that sea of being that is God. The reason we know Jesus practiced contemplative prayer is because the Gospels refer several times to his praying for a few hours at a time or going to a solitary place and praying all night long. Unless we imagine that his prayer list had become enormously long, it's impossible to imagine that he was doing verbal prayer all that time.

Beyond that, of course, Jesus, when asked, taught his disciples to pray, and it's the most famous prayer in the entire world; we call it the Lord's Prayer. I don't know if we can really imagine Jesus saying, "I want you to memorize this prayer and use it." Rather, I see the Lord's Prayer as more or less a summary of what we might pray for.

The contents of the Lord's Prayer are very interesting. After the initial "Our Father in heaven" and "hallowed be your name," it moves to a prayer for the coming of the kingdom: "Your kingdom come, your will be done, on earth as it is in heaven." At the heart of the Lord's Prayer is the petition for the coming of God's kingdom on earth; it's not about heaven. In fact, the Lord's Prayer doesn't say, "Help us to get to heaven." It's a very this-worldly prayer.

Then, of course, the next line is about bread: "Give us this day our daily bread." And for those of us who have plenty of bread, we perhaps hear that almost as a thank-you, an expression of gratitude, or perhaps even as meaning, "Keep giving us bread, as you've been doing." But this prayer was taught to a peasant audience, for whom bread, the material basis of life, was the central survival issue, so the coming of the kingdom of God means enough bread, enough food.

The next line is the one that we have to pause at if we visit another congregation, to see how they're going to say it: "Forgive us our trespasses, sins, debts." In two of the three versions of the Lord's Prayer that have come to us from the first century, the words are "debt" and "debtors" in both places. Debt was the other central survival issue of peasant life. So when Jesus was asked, "Teach us to pray," the prayer he responded with said the coming of God's kingdom meant enough food and mutual debt forgiveness. So in that respect the Lord's Prayer is very much focused on what we need for our lives in this world.

Many people view the Bible as the inerrant, literal word of God, but for many others this view of scripture is very problematic. You have written that seeing the Gospels as human products involves no denial of the reality of God or the presence of the Spirit in the process. Can you talk about this further?

I think the single most divisive issue in American Christianity today concerns the nature of the Bible. Many Christians, perhaps even a majority—I don't mean 98 percent, but more than half—are parts of Christian communities that affirm that the Bible is the inerrant Word of God, the infallible Word of God, and therefore factually and literally true in everything it says. This is the basis for the evolution-versus-creation controversy that's so prominent in the States. By the way, we're the only country in the world that even has a controversy like that. But, according to a number of polls I've seen, apparently half of American Christians believe that the universe and the earth are less than ten thousand years old.

Now, why is that? Is it because of invincible ignorance or the utter failure of our public school system? No, it's because a good number of Christians belong to churches that teach biblical inerrancy or infallibility, and they think you've got to deny science whenever it conflicts with something in the Bible.

It's important to remember that the notion of biblical inerrancy—that it's free from errors—is not the ancient teaching of the church. Biblical inerrancy and biblical infallibility are both mentioned for the first time in the second half of the 1600s and became relatively common in a stream of Protestantism only in the last century.

Fundamentalism, as a specifically named movement, began around 1910. I mention that because a good number of Christians as well as non-Christians think that believing in biblical inerrancy is orthodox Christianity. It's not at all; it's a modern development.

The alternative to biblical inerrancy and biblical infallibility is the recognition that the Bible is a human product. To say that it's a human product means something very simple, that it's the product of two ancient communities: the Hebrew Bible (the Jewish Bible, the Christian Old Testament) is the product of ancient Israel, and the New Testament is the product of the early Christian movement. The Bible tells us what our spiritual ancestors in those two ancient communities thought. It tells us about their experiences of the sacred. It tells us the stories they told about God. It tells us about what they thought life with God involved. It is their witness, their testimony. Our spiritual ancestors also canonized those documents; they declared them to be sacred, to be constitutive for religious identity and self-understanding.

To be Christian means to accept that this is our primary collection of documents, but it does not mean believing that they're inerrant, infallible, or to be interpreted literally. The Bible is full of poetry; it's full of hymns. It also, of course, has many stories and narratives. But to insist on a literal interpretation of these not only raises questions like, "What's the literal meaning of a poem?" and

"What's the literal meaning of a hymn?" It also creates unnecessary problems by insisting that stories, like the story of the talking snake in the third chapter of Genesis, really happened. It creates an unnecessary intellectual stumbling block.

If we ran into a story in any other literature in the world with a talking snake and two magic trees—a tree of the knowledge of good and evil, a tree of life—we would instantly recognize that as a symbolic narrative, a metaphorical narrative, or a myth, if you will. It's important to add: poetry can be true, but it's poetic truth. Myths can be true, but it's mythical truth.

Here German novelist Thomas Mann's definition of "myth" is wonderful. Thomas Mann says, "A myth is a story about the way things never were but always are." There never was a Garden of Eden. There never was a talking snake. Yet that story, understood mythically and symbolically, is a story about the way things always are. The Fall happens again and again and again. So when people talk about biblical inerrancy, they might be genuinely coming from a place of utter sincerity. They might think taking the Bible seriously means saying it's inerrant, but, ironically, to affirm biblical inerrancy and biblical literalism often involves not taking the Bible seriously at all.

Can you talk about the distinction between the pre-Easter and post-Easter Jesus, and why it's important to see those differently?

It's very helpful to realize that the word "Jesus" refers to two quite different, even though related, realities, and to distinguish between the two I refer to the pre-Easter Jesus and the post-Easter Jesus.

The "pre-Easter Jesus" is Jesus before his death, a flesh-and-blood historical figure who was maybe 5 foot 1 and probably weighed 110 pounds—we don't know that, but that's the average size of a man in that world. He had to eat and drink and was flesh like us, no different in kind from you and me. This is what the tradition means when it speaks of Jesus as fully human.

The "post-Easter Jesus" refers to what Jesus became after his death, and this Jesus is a spiritual reality. Let me underline that for some people that sounds like he's less than a physical reality, but that's because of the modern prejudice that the physical is real and the spiritual is questionable. When I say the post-Easter Jesus is a spiritual reality, I mean that he has all the qualities of God. He is "one with God," in the language of the New Testament. He can be experienced anywhere and in more than one place at the same time. And, unlike the pre-Easter Jesus, he doesn't have to eat and drink. He's not 5 foot 1 and 110 pounds. It would be ridiculous to think along these lines.

The reason this distinction matters is that if we don't make it, we tend to project the divine qualities of the post-Easter Jesus back onto the pre-Easter Jesus, and then he becomes an unreal human being. A lot of Christians think that Jesus was God walking around as a human being, and we even think that that's orthodox Christian belief.

But to think of the pre-Easter Jesus as God means he's not one of us. It also raises the question, "What does it mean to say that he is God?" Do we mean that he had the mind of God and that's why he knew stuff, so you could have asked him what the capital of Kansas was and he would've gotten it right? What would it mean to say that Jesus was God? Do we mean he had the power of God, so he could do anything? All of those conundrums obscure how utterly remarkable a human being Jesus was.

The South African Gospel and Jesus scholar Albert Nolan says, "Jesus is a much underrated man." To deny his humanity to him is to deny his greatness. When I say the pre-Easter Jesus was fully human, not different in kind from you and me, for me that in no way diminishes how remarkable he is. I oftentimes say the pre-Easter Jesus was one of the two most remarkable people who ever lived. Of course, somebody always asks me, "Who's the other one?" And I always say, "I really don't care." I'm simply making the point that what we see in Jesus is a human possibility.

One final way of making this same point: I sometimes speak of the pre-Easter Jesus as St. Francis with an exclamation point. I choose St. Francis because many think of him as the greatest and even the most Christlike of the Christian saints. Is St. Francis a human possibility? Of course. How often does a St. Francis come along? Not very often.

So I do see the pre-Easter Jesus as utterly remarkable. I see him as so open to the Spirit of God that he could be filled with it to a remarkable degree, but he's not *God simpliciter*. To say that, I think, creates confusion. To say that the pre-Easter Jesus is God or even simply that he was divine makes it impossible to say that we are to follow him. We as human beings cannot follow somebody who was not fully human himself.

One of your many books is titled The Heart of Christianity. *The concept of Christianity and being a Christian has different meanings for different people. Can you explain to us what you consider to be the essence or heart of Christianity, and what it means to be a Christian?*

I have a number of shorthand ways of speaking about what it means to be a Christian for me and, I think, more generally too. One of them simply goes like this. To be a Christian is to enter more and more deeply into a relationship with God as known decisively in Jesus.

The first part of that, "to enter more and more deeply into a relationship with God," would apply to the majority of the major religions of the world. What makes that a Christian statement is the last part, "as known decisively in Jesus"; Christians are people who find the decisive revelation of God in this person. Another way I have of putting it is to say that Christians are people who speak Christian.

I need to explain that a bit. I think of the religions of the world as a little bit like ethnic groups. French people are people who speak French, but it's not just about speaking French; there's a French ethos that goes with it. So if I were to become fluent in French, it would not really make me French, because I wouldn't have been steeped in that whole culture.

Similarly, you could speak Christian and not be Christian, but to a considerable extent being Christian means using Christian language and Christian scriptures to talk about God and our relationship to God and then, of course, following the path indicated by that language.

One final shorthand way of putting it is, Christians are those who live out their lives with God within the framework of the Christian tradition. Muslims are those who live out their lives with God within the framework of Islam. Jews are those who live out their lives with God within the framework of the Jewish tradition. And so on.

For me personally—and this is not about the superiority of Christianity at all; this is just why I am so deeply committed to the Christian journey—I think the Christian message, the Christian gospel, speaks to the two deepest yearnings of most human beings. One of those yearnings is for a fuller connection to what is. I think most people would say the best moments in their lives are those moments when they've felt most connected to what is right in front of their face.

I also think that most people yearn for the world to be a better place. These two yearnings are at the heart of the Christian message. The first is the yearning for God. The second is the yearning for a better world that is expressed in the second great commandment, to love your neighbor as yourself. For me, being Christian provides a vehicle, a vessel, a community for living out those yearnings.

Chapter 14

The Heart and Soul of Christianity

URING MY INTRODUCTION, I was sitting there thinking about my having written *The Heart of Christianity,* Huston's having written *The Soul of Christianity,*
and Huston's seeing that book as a corrective of mine. I
thought perhaps I should just break into song with a few
verses of "Heart and Soul"!

Humor aside, I want to begin with a brief tribute to
Huston Smith. I need to be careful here, because I could

Lecture with Huston Smith given at the First Congregational
Church, Berkeley, California, November 10, 2006.

go on quite long. Like many of you, I've known about Huston's work for forty years, probably. But I first met Huston some twenty-one years ago, when he was the leader of a National Endowment for the Humanities seminar here in Berkeley for eight weeks, and I was one of fifteen participants with him. That marked the beginning of what I am pleased to say is a friendship, and it's such an honor, such a treat, for me to have done a number of events like this with Huston over the years and to be doing yet another one tonight.

I have sometimes said that when I grow up, I want to be like Huston Smith. I figure it'll take me a few more incarnations to get there, but that's all right. I also want to say that I've learned more from Huston than from any other scholar outside of my area of specialization. I find myself on the same page as him on everything of importance that I can think of. And he has also helped me to find that page.

Let me turn now to what I see as most central to Christianity, what I see as the heart of Christianity. I will develop five main points.

The Reality of the Sacred

First: at the heart of Christianity is *a robust affirmation of God or the sacred or Spirit*—terms that I use synonymously and interchangeably. I stress "robust," because I think in Western Christianity over the last few hundred years that affirmation has sometimes been a bit tentative or uncertain.

That has happened in what we sometimes refer to as liberal Christianity as well as in conservative Christianity. In liberal Christianity, a whole cohort of seminarians including my generation, and maybe a generation on either side of mine, came out of seminary with a lot of uncertainty about whether God was real. This may have been due to seminary, but it also could have been the times. It wasn't too long ago that the "death of God" theology was very current.

Conservative Christians in the West have also oftentimes suffered from uncertainty about God, and that's why there's been so much emphasis on believing in God. People take it for granted you can't know God, so when you can't know something and everything's uncertain, then of course that's why it takes faith. So even with those who say they're most certain about God because they believe in God really strongly, there's a kind of tentativeness to that, because it's primarily about believing in a reality who, from one point of view, may or may not exist. So I want to stress that God should not be thought of as a problematic reality who may or may not exist. As Paul Tillich remarked half a century ago, "If, when you use the word 'God,' you are thinking of a being who may or may not exist, then you are not thinking of God."

For me personally, God is more real than the world is, not because I've talked myself into that, but because there have been moments when I feel as though I have sensed—and I mean that quite literally, with the senses—the reality of God. Of course, affirming the reality of the sacred does not differentiate Christianity from the other religions. It shares this in common with all of the other enduring religions of the world, and it is central to what Huston calls the "primordial tradition," which, reduced to its simplest form, affirms a two-tiered understanding of reality: the visible world of our ordinary experience and a nonmaterial realm charged with energy and power upon which the visible world is dependent for its existence in every moment of time.

Those of you who are Buddhists may disagree. About the statement that Buddhism affirms the reality of the sacred, some Buddhists would say to me, "We don't believe in God." Fair enough. But I must admit that I find it difficult to distinguish Buddhist such-ness from Christian is-ness. If that's opaque to you, you can ask about that.

Sources of Revelation

Second main point: How do we know about God? What are the *sources of revelation* that are at the heart of Christianity? For Christians, there are two primary sources of revelation, both of them referred to as the "Word of God": the Word of God as known in the *Bible* and the Word of God as known in *Jesus*. Finding the decisive sources of revelation in the Bible and Jesus is what makes Christians Christian and not Jewish or Muslim and so forth.

Now, to say a bit more about these two sources of revelation. The Bible as the Word of God—and notice that it's capital *W* singular—is expressed in human words. I want to stress that the Bible is a human product. To think of the Bible as a divine product, in the sense of being perfect, infallible, and inerrant, is basically a modern Christian heresy. Nobody's pronounced it a heresy, but the first time that the Bible was ever spoken of as inerrant and infallible was in the second half of the 1600s. So we have the Word of God in human words, and the Christian tradition has declared these human words—the Bible—to be sacred revelation. But those words must always be understood as pointing beyond themselves, not as the absolute themselves.

The other source of revelation for Christians is Jesus, as the Word of God embodied in a human person. The Bible, the Word of God expressed in human words. Jesus, the Word of God embodied in a person, in language from the New Testament, the Word become flesh, the Word incarnate. One of the insights that I owe to Huston, and it's one of those things that, as soon as you hear it, you think, "Of course! Should have thought of that myself," is that Christianity is the only major religion that finds the decisive revelation of God in a person. That's not a claim to superiority; it's a marker of difference.

This leads to the next point about the two sources of revelation: *the supremacy of Jesus.* For Christians, the meaning of our Christological language—Jesus as Son of God, Word of God, Light of the World, and so forth—is that Jesus is the decisive revelation, disclosure, epiphany of God, more precisely and specifically, what can be seen of God in a human life. There is much of God that can't be seen in a human life: infinity, omnipresence, omniscience—none of those things can be seen in a human life. What can be seen of God in a human life is the character of God—what God is like—and the passion of God—what God is most passionate about. I suppose the older language for the character and passion of God is the nature and will of God. For Christians, Jesus is the decisive disclosure of God's character and of passion. And when Jesus and the Bible conflict, as they sometimes do, Jesus is decisive. I sometimes express this colloquially by saying orthodox Christianity affirms that Jesus trumps the Bible. And it's been so from the beginning.

How do we interpret this revelation? In two words, historically and metaphorically. By historically, I mean we interpret the revelation in its ancient historical context. It doesn't mean trying to determine how much of what is reported really happened; it means determining what these stories and these texts meant within the ancient communities that told these stories and produced these texts. By metaphorically, I mean the more than literal, the more than historical meaning of these stories and texts. To use a phrase from a contemporary Roman Catholic theologian, David Tracy, from the University of Chicago, a metaphorical reading enables us to get at "the surplus of meaning that the text carries."

Not only do I think the Bible should be interpreted historically and metaphorically, but so also Jesus should be understood historically and metaphorically. By historically, I mean we need to understand Jesus in his first-century context, or we miss so much of what he is about. By metaphorically, I mean that Jesus and his teachings have a meaning that transcends that first-century context. One might express this in speaking of Jesus as the "parable of God" or the "metaphor of God." But both a historical and metaphorical approach apply to Jesus as well.

A Path, a Way

Third main point: *Christianity is "the way."* I don't mean that in the sense of Christian exclusivism, but that, for Christians, Christianity is "the way"—it is a path. Let me briefly tell you a story to illustrate this point. I fly a lot. Last week, I hit a million real miles on the airline that I use most. For me, flying is about R and R: it's about rest and reading. So I assiduously seek to avoid conversations with the person sitting next to me. I try not to be rude, but I try not to give a seatmate much of an inroad, because you can sometimes get a chatty person.

I was actually reading Huston Smith's book *Why Religion Matters* on a flight a couple years ago, and the woman sitting next to me looked at the title of the book and said, "Oh! You're interested in religion!"

I said, "Yeah," trying to leave it at that.

And she said, "I'm very interested in Buddhism and Sufism, because they're both about a way, but I don't have much interest in Christianity, because it's all about believing."

I understood her point immediately, even as I silently disagreed with it. For most modern Western Christians, believing is at the very center of what it means to be Christian: either you believe or you don't. That's a modern emphasis, once again. The earliest name for Christianity in the New Testament was followers of "the Way" (Acts 9:1). And, of course, the notion of "a way" is a cross-cultural, indeed archetypal image. Buddhism is about a way, Taoism is about a way, and so forth. Christianity is also about a way, a path of transformation.

And that path has two dimensions to it, equally important in the Bible. One is a personal dimension; it's about personal transformation. New Testament imagery for that is dying and rising with Christ, understood as a metaphor for an internal process of transformation. It's being born again, entering into a new identity and a new way of being.

Second, this transformation is political. It's about the transformation of the world, and this is expressed in the New Testament with the central phrase the "kingdom of God." The kingdom of God is what life would be like on earth if God were king and the rulers of this world were not. The kingdom of God is for the earth. In the Lord's Prayer we pray, "Thy kingdom come on earth." Or, to use the most famous verse in the New Testament to make that point, "For God so loved the world." It doesn't say "For God so loved me" or "For God so loved us" or "For God so loved the church" or "For God so loved the elect" or "For God so loved Christians," but "For God so loved the world," which I hear as not only including human beings, but the nonhuman world as well. Once one sees Christianity as a way, it means that practice—which means paying attention to the reality of God and our relationship with God—practice, not believing, is central.

A last comment as I leave the third point: the way is symbolized within Christianity preeminently by the cross. The cross is a symbol of the path of personal transformation—"I have been crucified with Christ; and it is no longer I who live, but it is Christ who lives in me," words from Paul (Gal. 2:19–20)—and also the symbol of confrontation with the powers that rule this world. The cross is both personal and political.

Community

Fourth point: at the heart of Christianity is *community*. Can you be a solitary Christian? Yes. But in an age of individualism, we've got to watch that, especially if our motive for being a solitary Christian is that we can't stand other Christians. But community is utterly central to Christianity, as it is once again to all of the enduring religions. Community of praise, community as nourishment. I'm a flaming introvert, off the scale, and yet the most nourishing thing I can do for my Christian journey is to be part of a worshipping community that sings its heart out. I even find contemplative prayer, which you would think of as the most solitary kind of experience—after all, you're silent—more powerful when I do it with a group of people than when I do it by myself. I don't know why, but it underlines community as utterly central.

And then there's community as a community of formation—Christian community as a community of resocialization into a new identity and way of being. We all, or at least most of us, have been socialized into modern Western culture and most of us into an American form of modern Western culture. I don't need to trash modern Western culture or the American way of life, but the central values of Western life over the last hundred years are so radically different from anything that is recognizably Christian that to be Christian means to be resocialized into a different vision and a different way of being. Christian community is a vehicle or agent of that resocialization. I once described the three primary values of the American way of life as the three *A*s: appearance, affluence, and achievement. Think of how different those are from anything that is identifiably Christian. That's, to some extent, what we stand against.

Authentic Christianity

Fifth and finally: in my judgment, there should be *an edginess to authentic Christianity*. The use of the adjective "authentic" is, perhaps, questionable there—what makes Christianity authentic?—but I'm simply referring to the Christianity of our founding figures and texts: early Christianity, Jesus, Paul, and so forth. To say the obvious, for those of us who are Christian, we have a crucified Lord—think about it! We all know this, but what does it mean to follow a crucified Lord? To follow a person who was executed by the authorities, who was executed by the ruling powers of his time, the domination system of his time, the powers of this world, and maybe the best empire of the ancient world. The powers of this world killed Jesus and God vindicated him, which is one of the central meanings of Easter. Good Friday and Easter: executed by empire, vindicated by God. In the language of the book of Acts, Peter's said to the authorities: "God has made him both Lord and Christ, this Jesus whom you crucified" (2:36).

To say the obvious, Christianity over the centuries has often become too comfortable with culture, pretty much from the time when it became the dominant religion of Europe, too embedded in convention, too wedded to this world, so it's been difficult to distinguish conventional morality from what it means to be Christian. But I'm convinced there are times when it needs to become edgy, critical of the dominant culture, and affirmative of an alternate vision grounded in God's passion for the well-being of the world. The message of authentic Christianity is that there is a better world and that better world, for the New Testament, is not primarily about heaven. There's no denial of an afterlife in what I'm saying, but the better world we're talking about is to occur on earth. "Your kingdom come on earth," we pray. It's especially important for us in our time to take seriously the edginess of Christianity, especially for those of us who are American Christians. What does it mean to be a Christian and a citizen of empire? Or, in Dorothee Soelle's provocative phrase of fifteen years ago or so, "What does it mean to be a member of Pharaoh's household and a Christian?"

Summary

I leave you with two very brief definitions of how I would characterize what a Christian is. First, at the center of the Christian life is a transforming relationship with God as known decisively in Jesus. If I were defining Jewish life, I would say that at its center is a transforming relationship with God as known decisively in Torah. The same applies to other religions. Finally, a Christian is somebody who lives the way within the framework of the Christian tradition, just as living within the Jewish tradition makes one Jewish and doing so within the Islamic tradition makes one Muslim, and so forth. There's no claim that one of these is intrinsically better than the others, but there's nothing terribly complex about defining what a Christian is. Christians are those who live out their relationship with God within the framework of this tradition.

Chapter 15

Encountering the Wisdom
of Other Faiths

THE TITLE OF MY LECTURE TONIGHT IS "Seeing Religions Again: Religious Pluralism" or "Religious Pluralism: Seeing Religions Again." And to give you a brief road map up front, there will be four main parts. In part one, I'm going to speak briefly about the fact of religious pluralism. In part two, I'm going to suggest a way of seeing religions. In part three, some comments about the similarities and differences among the religions. And then in part

---

Lecture at the University of California, San Diego, January 2002.

four, Christians and the issue of pluralism or, alternately, being Christian in an age of pluralism.

The Fact of Pluralism

I begin with part one, the *fact of pluralism*. To say the obvious, we live in an age of religious pluralism. Awareness of other religions and other cultural traditions is one of the central features of our time. To make this point, I want to refer to an important recent book—also highly readable—by Diana Eck, a professor at Harvard University and director of the Pluralism Project. The title of the book is *A New Religious America*. Let me briefly report to you some of the data she includes in that book about religious pluralism.

The central argument of the book is that religious pluralism, or religious diversity, is a fact of American life. The United States has recently and rapidly become the world's most religiously diverse nation. The 1965 Immigration Act opened up immigration to people from nations outside of Europe, and the twofold result over the last thirty-five years has been, first, a dramatic increase in immigration from Asia, the Middle East, and to a lesser extent Africa and, second, a dramatic growth in the number of people in the States practicing religions other than Christianity and Judaism. Some of these folks are new immigrants, but many of them have been born in the United States as children of the first wave of immigrants that began in 1965. Thus, religious diversity or pluralism is not simply an intellectual issue within the academic study of religion; it is a cultural reality that Americans, as citizens of a historically Christian, Jewish, and secular nation, need to become aware of.

Among the evidence that Diana Eck cites: there are six million Muslim Americans. There are thus more Muslim Americans than the combined total of Episcopalians and Presbyterians—Episcopalians somewhat over two million, Presbyterians somewhat over three million. There are about the same number of Muslim Americans as Jewish Americans. There are four million American Buddhists; the majority of these are recent immigrants and American-born children of Buddhist immigrants, but there are also a fair number of North American—"European," as it were—converts to Buddhism. Thus, there are more Buddhists in the United States than either Episcopalians or Presbyterians.

In lesser numbers, there are about a million Hindus, about as many as there are members of the United Church of Christ, and there are about three hundred thousand Sikhs. The phenomenon of religious pluralism, religious diversity, is not confined to major metropolitan areas; it is found in regional and even small cities. Eck writes about a huge white mosque in Toledo, Ohio; a great Hindu temple in Nashville, Tennessee; a Cambodian Buddhist monastery in the farmlands of Minnesota; a Sikh gurdwara in Fremont, California; Muslim, Hindu, and Buddhist temples in Salt Lake City and Dallas; Cambodian Buddhist communities in Iowa and Oklahoma; Tibetan Buddhist retreat centers in Vermont and Colorado; and many more. Her conclusion is that the American religious landscape is changing very dramatically in our time. To quote her directly, "This is an astonishing new reality. We have never been here before."

Now, this is very different from the world that I grew up in and that anybody in my generation grew up in. I grew up in a small town in North Dakota—probably not a representative sample of the United States, to be sure, but I think everybody in that town of fourteen hundred people would have identified themselves as Christian, and we certainly had no Buddhists or Jews or Muslims. Or, to use an example that goes beyond small-town North Dakota, in the middle 1950s, a scholar named Bill Herberg wrote a very well known book for the time about religious diversity in America. What's interesting is the title of the book, *Protestant, Catholic, and Jew*. Fifty years ago, that's what religious diversity in the United States meant. The change is dramatic, and thus there is a need, an imperative to understand other religions—an imperative that has been made more forced and urgent by the events of September 11.

The issue of religious pluralism is not simply a theoretical one about religions that we've heard of but might never encounter, but an immensely practical one. For those of us in this society who are Christians, being aware of religious pluralism and other religions can, it seems to me, enrich our understanding of Christianity and what it means to be Christian. I am persuaded that we see Christianity—its nature and purpose—more clearly when we see it within the framework of religious pluralism. Religious pluralism can help us understand our own tradition better. To refer again to Diana Eck, this time paraphrasing her, Eck says whoever knows only one religion is unlikely to understand what religion is about.

Seeing Religions Again

I turn to part two: *seeing religions again.* Here I'm going to provide a compact introduction to the nature and function of religions—and note I'm using the plural—the essence and purpose of religions. I'm going to suggest how we might see the major religions of the world and thus also how to see Christianity. I will describe a general understanding of religions with six statements, all six statements commonly affirmed within the academic study of religion—that is, there'd be widespread agreement among religious scholars about these statements.

First statement about religions: *Religions are cultural-linguistic traditions.* Pretty abstract, but it's actually a helpful definition. I owe this language to George Lindbeck, of Yale Divinity School. I'm not sure it's original with him, but in his work is where I encountered it. What it means is that each religion originates within a particular culture and thus uses the language and symbols of that culture. Moreover, if a religion survives for any length of time, and all of the major religions have, it becomes a cultural-linguistic tradition in its own right. That is, it becomes a way of construing the world, of structuring the world, and with its own particular language and symbols.

Thus being Christian, or Jewish, or Muslim is a little bit like being French or Italian. To be French means not only knowing French; it means knowing something about the ethos of being French, it means to have lived within a French world and to have had that world structure your vision of life. Of course, there's a sense in which being religious is different from this, because it's a much more universal identity, one that transcends national, racial, and ethnic boundaries. But, nevertheless, it's very helpful to think of religions as cultural-linguistic traditions, each with its own language, symbols, and so on.

Second statement about religions: *Religions are human constructions.* Religions are human constructions, or human products. This is a corollary of the first statement. As cultural-linguistic traditions, religions are human creations. Within that I'm including their scriptures (thus for Christians the Bible is a human product), their teachings, their doctrines, their rituals, their practices—all of these are human creations, human constructions. This time I use a phrase from a Harvard religious scholar, Gordon Kaufman. Kaufman speaks of religions as "imaginative human constructions." He doesn't use "imaginative" in a negative sense, as when we say something sounds really far-fetched. He means imaginative as both creative and using the language of the imagination, the language of images, symbols, story, and so forth.

Now, not all religious people would agree with the statement that religions are human products or human constructions. Within the three major Western religions, the Abrahamic traditions, as they are commonly called, there are many who would say that their religion comes from God, that it's a divine and not a human product. I think you are all aware that official Muslim teaching is that the Qur'an was dictated by Allah to Muhammad. Within Judaism, Orthodox Jews typically affirm that the Torah—both the laws given to Moses on Mt. Sinai that are included in the Pentateuch and the oral Torah—was given directly by God to Moses. And fundamentalist Christians typically claim that the Bible is a divine product and thus infallible and inerrant. But within the framework of the academic study of religion, these claims look like a common human tendency to ground a sacred tradition in God. That is, lots of religious traditions say, "Our tradition comes from God." In fact, this is one of the things that is characteristic of religions—they tend to ground their traditions in divine origin.

Those first two statements both stress the human origins of religion, but the third statement brings God back into the picture. *Religions are responses to the experience of the sacred*—or God or the Spirit, terms I use synonymously and interchangeably. I take the reality of God very seriously; I am utterly convinced that there is a "more"—to use William James's marvelously generic term for the sacred—a stupendous, wondrous more. I'm convinced that this "more" has been experienced in every human culture and that the origin of the major religious traditions lies in the experiences of the "more." So I see religions as human products, but human products created in response to the experience of the sacred in the particular culture in which each emerges.

Fourth statement: *Religions are wisdom traditions.* I owe this statement to a man I'm honored to call my friend, Huston Smith. He speaks about this a lot, that religions are wisdom traditions. Wisdom in both religion and philosophy is concerned with the question, "How shall I live? What is life about?" Well, this is what the religions to a large extent are about: they are disclosures about how to live—and by that I don't mean just morals, but something more comprehensive. They are disclosures about life and reality. And it's not just that those disclosures are individual responses to the questions; they are the accumulated wisdom of the past of centuries of thinkers, which range from very practical wisdom to theological and metaphysical wisdom. The religions are a treasure trove of wisdom.

Fifth statement: *Religions are means of ultimate transformation.* I owe this short statement to Frederick Strang, author of an introduction to religion textbook published some twenty-five years ago or so. Let me unpack that definition. Religions are means in the sense that they have a very practical purpose, and that practical purpose is ultimate transformation. When we speak of ultimate transformation, we mean not just psychological transformation, important as that is, but spiritual transformation,

transformation of the self at its deepest level. That is the very practical purpose of religion. That transformation is from an old way of being to a new way of being, from an old identity to a new identity, and the fruit or product of this transformation across religious traditions is compassion, becoming more compassionate beings. This is central to all the major religions, and the saints of the various traditions look very similar in this respect.

And sixth and finally: *Religions are sacraments of the sacred.* Let me define the word "sacrament" here. Those of us who are Christians are familiar with the two universal sacraments of the Protestant and Catholic traditions and then the five additional sacraments of the Catholic tradition itself. But I'm using the word "sacrament" in a broader sense. A sacrament is a mediator of the sacred, or a sacrament is a mediator of the Spirit. A sacrament is anything finite and visible through which the Spirit becomes present to us. In this broad sense, nature can be a sacrament, music can be a sacrament. Virtually everything in human history has, for somebody, been a means whereby the Spirit has been mediated. To apply this definition to religions: the purpose of religions is to mediate the sacred. The purpose of their scriptures, their rituals, their practices is to become a vehicle or vessel for the sacred to become present to us.

If we take this seriously, it also has an effect upon what we think being religious means. Within the Christian tradition over the last three hundred years, especially for Protestants, but also for Catholics, because of the effect of the Enlightenment on Western Christianity, there's been an enormous emphasis on believing. Being a Christian means believing in the Bible, in Jesus, in God, or in Christianity. If you see religion as a sacrament, the point is not to believe in the sacrament; the point is to live within the tradition and let the sacrament do its work within you, let the sacrament mediate the reality of the sacred to you. It seems to me that this is the purpose of the Buddhist tradition, the Muslim tradition, the Jewish tradition, and so forth, that they are means whereby the sacred becomes present to and works within people.

Similarities and Differences Among the Religions

I turn now to part three. If you reflect on the similarities and differences between religions, you arrive at the very simple, very elementary conclusion: *Religions are both alike and different.* I've already touched on this somewhat by speaking of the six characteristics the religions have in common. But to say a bit more about their commonality, I want to mention four things here. First, they are grounded in *experiences of the sacred.* This is most obvious with the mystical strand of each religious tradition—the mystical strand is the most experiential of each tradition, and the mystical strands of the various religions are very similar to each other.

Second, they're very alike in the *paths* that they teach. Most religions have a path, a "way" at the center of their message. This is perhaps most apparent in Buddhism, which speaks of the Eightfold Path, but teaching about the way or the path is also utterly central to the Christian tradition. The earliest name of the Christian tradition was, according to the book of Acts, "the Way" (2:36). The paths that the religions teach are remarkably similar. Within the Christian tradition, it's symbolized by the cross as a metaphor for the internal, psychological, spiritual process of transformation—namely, dying to an old way of being and being born to a new way of being, dying to an old identity and being born into a new identity. At the center of the Buddhist way or path is letting go, which means letting go of one's prior understanding of who one is and what life is about and being born into a new understanding of all of that, not just a cognitive, intellectual understanding, but a new way of being. It's also central to the Muslim tradition. The word "Islam" itself means "submission," meaning radical centering in God and therefore not centering in culture or tradition or yourself. In the Muslim tradition, one of the sayings attributed to Muhammad is, "Die before you die." That's the same thing as death and resurrection as a metaphor for a process that happens in the midst of this life: "Die before you die."

Third, the religions are very similar in their characteristic *practices*. Perhaps the most characteristic practices of religion are worship and prayer. Fourth, they're very similar in the kind of life that results, namely, a *life of compassion*.

Does seeing all of these similarities mean that the religions are all basically the same? No, it doesn't. They are very different. They're as different as the cultures and histories that shaped them. They're as different as the cultural-linguistic traditions in which they were born and the cultural-linguistic traditions they became in their own right. Let me speak briefly now about three ways of understanding their similarities and differences using the work of three scholars who have spoken about this. They end up saying very similar things. The first of these is Williams James, in his magnificent book *The Varieties of Religious Experience*—now one hundred years old.

By the way, back in 1999 when lists were being compiled of the most important books of the twentieth century, William James's *The Varieties of Religious Experience* appeared at number two on the list of the one hundred most important nonfiction books, which is very impressive, and it's still marvelous to read. In his wonderful concluding chapter, one of the richest chapters in religious scholarship that I know of, one of the topics that James deals with is the similarities and differences between religions. He says they are most similar in three of the respects I mentioned earlier. They are most similar in the kinds of experiences reported within each religion, experiences of the sacred, in the practices they enjoin, and in the behavior that results—once again, compassion.

James goes on to say they are most different in their beliefs and doctrines, in their conceptualizations, if you will. When you think about it, that makes perfect sense, for beliefs and doctrines—that is, concepts that are shaped into religious teachings—are most affected by culture, most reflect the particularities of the culture in which they come into existence.

The second scholar whose work I want to refer to as an aid in thinking about similarities and differences is René Guénon (1886–1951). In speaking of religion, Guénon makes a distinction between esoteric core and exoteric form. The esoteric, or internal, core of religion is really that experiential core that lies at the heart of each religion. The exoteric form is the external forms of the religions—their scriptures, institutions, beliefs, and so forth. His claim, identical to James's but using this different language, is that the esoteric core—I think Guénon would even say the mystical core—of each of the major religions is very similar and perhaps identical. It is in their exoteric forms that they differ.

The third scholar is one I mentioned briefly before: Huston Smith. Huston Smith speaks of the "primordial tradition." By that phrase he means a tradition going back to the beginnings, I think he'd even say of humanity, but certainly going back to the beginnings of the religious traditions. It's not only primordial in that it goes back to the beginnings, but also, he argues, because a common understanding underlies all of the enduring religions of the world. Smith finds that there are two elements in this common, underlying understanding. First, there is a multilayered understanding of reality—namely, that in addition to the visible world of our ordinary experience, there are nonmaterial levels of reality. Second, there is also a multilayered understanding of the self—body, mind, soul, spirit. He finds this multilayered understanding of the self to be the conceptual heart of every one of the religious traditions.

For all of these scholars, then, what the religions share in common is this internal core of experience. Now I want to make two comments about the external forms—the differences. The first of these comments is that these external forms matter. We have a tendency to think that if all religions have this internal core in common, then that's the point of unification, and if we could just drop the external forms, we'd be a lot better off. One often finds this expressed in the common statement of our time: "I'm not religious, but I'm spiritual." "Religion" here means the institution, the teachings, the tradition, the external form, and it is set in opposition to spirituality, the experiential core.

I don't doubt that a person can be spiritual without being religious, but what I want to challenge is the opposition between those two, because it seems to me—and here I'm indebted to Huston Smith—that religion, still meaning the institution, teachings, tradition, and so forth, is the way that spirituality gets traction within history. Religions are to spirituality what schools, colleges, and universities are to education. You can become a self-educated person by avoiding all institutions of higher learning, but it's really like inventing the wheel every generation.

So the first way in which I would say the external forms matter is that they are meant to be vehicles of wisdom, vessels through which the Spirit speaks to us and operates within us. A second way in which the external forms matter is when they matter too much. This is the downside, when the external forms are overemphasized; that is, when being Christian or Muslim or Jewish means believing this set of beliefs and not that set of beliefs. When the external forms are emphasized, or made central, then the differences between religions become more apparent than their similarities.

And when the external forms—the scriptures and doctrines—are absolutized, as they are in religious fundamentalism, then religious exclusivism is the inevitable result. Religious dialogue basically becomes impossible if the external forms are absolutized. Conversion becomes the goal, and conflict is often the result. So the external forms matter, but they matter precisely as relative expressions, as vehicles of the sacred and not as absolutes in themselves.

Being Christian in an Age of Pluralism

I turn to part four: the implications of religious pluralism for Christians. Here I will speak very directly about how I as a Christian see this. My first point in this section is the need to reject Christian exclusivism. I'm not pretending this is a dogmatic pronouncement from God—this is how I see it. But I see it strongly this way. What I mean by Christian exclusivism is, I suspect, apparent to all of you. It's what I, and I suspect many of us in the church, grew up with. Christian exclusivism says Jesus is the only way of salvation, Christianity is the only true religion, and it's important to convert the world to Christianity, because souls are perishing, lost in shades of night. Christian exclusivism has been part of conventional Christian teaching for centuries. There's no denying that. I don't think it's the authentic voice of the tradition, by the way, but it's been part of conventional Christianity for centuries.

Within the Roman Catholic Church, it's been expressed using the Latin phrase *Extra ecclesiam nulla salus est,* "Outside of the church there is no salvation." And, of course, after the Reformation, the Roman Catholic tradition understood that to mean that even Protestants are out of luck—not just non-Christians, but all non-Catholics are out of luck. The Second Vatican Council radically changed that and actually openly affirmed that God is known in all of the religious traditions of the world. The Vatican may be backpedaling on that right now; it's hard to know what the next few years will disclose.

Protestants, of course, rejected that Catholic notion— partly because it rejected them—and we Protestants said, "No, there's salvation outside of the Catholic Church; there's salvation through Jesus, but only through Jesus, and of course we've got Jesus." So it ended up being the same thing. As I just mentioned, I grew up with this, but I now see things very differently. I can no longer affirm that Christianity is the only way of salvation. There's more than one reason I can't; I mention three.

The first reason might be called common sense. When you think about the claim that Christianity is the only way of salvation, it's a pretty strange notion. Does it make sense that the Creator of the whole world has chosen to be known in only one religious tradition, which just fortunately happens to be our own? Some Christians would make that even narrower, that it's only their own particular version of the Christian tradition that conveys saving truth.

A second reason is that it's very difficult to reconcile Christian exclusivism with the Christian emphasis on grace. God's radical grace means God's unconditional acceptance of all of us. But if one must be a Christian to be in right relationship with God, that's a requirement. And suddenly we're talking about requirements, not about grace, about law, not about grace. The third reason I can't accept the Christian exclusivism of my youth is my experience: my study of other religions and my acquaintance with people of other religious traditions. It now seems clear to me that God, or the sacred, or the Spirit is known in all of the enduring religious traditions and not simply in our own. If I thought I had to believe that Christianity was the only way, I could not be a Christian.

Moreover, to turn to the upside of this, it seems to me that seeing the similarities between Christianity and other religions adds to the credibility of Christianity rather than threatening it. When Christianity claims to be the only true religion, it loses much of its credibility. But when Christianity is seen as one of the great religions of the world, it has great credibility. The similarities, it seems to me, are cause for celebration and not to be resisted. All of that's my first point on being Christian in an age of pluralism.

My second point concerns the significance of Jesus for Christians within a pluralistic framework. I want to begin with the relatively few exclusivistic passages in the New Testament. There aren't very many of them, about three. I'm going to talk about the one that's most familiar. We must remember, though, that these passages that speak of salvation being only in the name of Jesus reflect the centrality and the utter decisiveness of Jesus in the lives of the early Christians. These statements that Jesus is the only way can be understood as exclamations of devotion flowing out of the experience of having found access to God through Jesus. "Jesus is the way that I have found, and he's the only way!"

John Hick, philosopher of religion and theologian at Claremont, suggests we understand this "only way" language as "the poetry of devotion and the hyperbole of the heart." And I love that, because it honors the genuine devotion and ecstatic sense of deliverance that lies behind those statements. Those statements are a little bit like the language that lovers use for each other, when the lover says to the beloved, "You're the most beautiful person in the world." It would be a wooden-headed literalist who, overhearing that, says, "Oh, I don't know. You know, cute maybe, but the most beautiful person in the world?" That's the hyperbole of the heart, that's the poetry of devotion, and it expresses honest, genuine feeling, but whenever one makes doctrine out of hyperbole, one is creating problems.

Let me turn to that best known of the exclusivistic passages, John 14:6, where, according to John, Jesus says, "I am the way, and the truth, and the life. No one comes to the Father except through me." To a lot of people, that sounds crystal clear: salvation is only through Jesus. But it's very important to ask about that verse, "What is the way that Jesus is?" Jesus is the incarnation of the way for John, just as he is the incarnation of the Word of God, the incarnation of the wisdom of God. He's the incarnation of the way, the embodiment of the way—well, what is the way that he embodies? For John, it's real clear—this is true for the rest of the New Testament too—the way that Jesus embodies is the path of death and resurrection. No one comes to God except by dying to an old way of being and being born into a new way of being, dying to an old identity and being born into a new identity. In this sense, Jesus is the embodiment of the way. If you think it really means you've got to know the name of Jesus in order to be saved, then we're almost talking about salvation by syllables. It's not about having the right words.

One of the best exemplifications of the point I'm making right now about John 14:6 is contained in a sermon preached at Boston University School of Theology, a Methodist seminary, in the 1950s, as I recall this story. A Hindu professor was preaching. He was on the faculty, and the lectionary text for the day that his turn came up to preach in chapel was John 14:1–8. He read the text out loud: "Jesus said, 'I am the way, and the truth, and the life. No one comes to God but by me.'" Then he looked out at the gathered community and said, "This verse is absolutely true. Jesus is the only way, and that way is known in every religion in the world." Which is to say, Jesus is the incarnation of the universal truth and universal path, not the incarnation of a unique and exclusive path unknown anywhere else.

The other point I want to make about Jesus in the context of religious pluralism is the significance of Jesus for Christians—I want to underline the utter centrality of Jesus for us as Christians. I don't think religious pluralism should make us start talking about Jesus as, you know, one of the lights, or something like that. I don't think we should water down what we say about Jesus in order to embrace religious diversity. Jesus is constitutive of Christian identity. Christians are people who find the decisive disclosure of God in Jesus, just as Muslims are people who find the decisive disclosure of God in the Qur'an and Jews are people who find the decisive disclosure of God in the Torah—that's what makes them Christian, Muslim, Jewish. We don't need to water that down at all. We can say Jesus is for us as Christians the decisive disclosure of God without needing to say that he's the only disclosure of God. We can say decisive—he's utterly central for us—without needing to deny the other religions.

Krister Stendahl, former dean of Harvard Divinity School, bishop of the Church of Sweden, New Testament scholar, and wonderful human being, gave a lecture last year in which, among other things, he talked about religious exclusivism and Jesus. Making a point very similar to the one I'm making, he said, "We can sing our love songs to Jesus with wild abandon without needing to tell dirty stories about other religions." What he meant by that was we can uphold the centrality of Jesus without dismissing other religions. But there's a positive point I want to make here: we can sing our love songs to Jesus with wild abandon, even while affirming that God is known in the other religious traditions.

Then my conclusion, quite brief: Why be Christian in an age of religious pluralism? I want to develop this point by reading to you an e-mail interchange I was involved in about six months ago. This basically friendly e-mail from somebody who'd been reading *Meeting Jesus Again for the First Time* included this question:

> In your research, you have been exposed to many different cultural traditions about religion and the effects on their followers, yet you say you are still a Christian. Why is that? Is there something about Jesus Christ that makes him different from all of the other religious leaders? Or is Jesus just one among the many of the world's religious leaders? I'm wondering what you have found unique in Jesus that keeps you in the Christian fold.

I responded as follows:

> Let me begin by describing how I define "Christian." It's very simple. A Christian is one who lives out his or her relationship with God within the framework of the Christian tradition, just as a Jew is one who does that in the Jewish

tradition, a Muslim is one who does that in the Islamic tradition, and so forth. I don't think God cares whether we are Christian, Jewish, or Muslim, and so forth. All our paths of relationship with God are paths of transformation.

So why, then, am I a Christian? In part, because being part of a religious tradition and religious community is important to me. I'm nourished by it. Though I think one can be in relationship with God apart from religious community, I experience so much richness in religious community that for me not to be part of one would be like refusing a banquet in the midst of hunger.

And why Christian, rather than Jewish or Buddhist? Not because I can make a case for the superiority of the Christian tradition, but, very simply, because for me the Christian tradition feels like home in a way that no other tradition could, in addition to which I find the Christian tradition extraordinarily rich—its antiquity, its wisdom, its beauty, and at its best its goodness. Finally, I do not see Jesus as unique, except in the sense that the Buddha and Muhammad both are unique—that is, not exactly like anybody else. Rather, I see him as the incarnation of a universal truth that is also known in other traditions—

namely, he discloses what God is like and what a life full of God is like.

Q & A

STUDENT: *I don't get the transforming thing. It isn't just learning and trying to be good or like Jesus, Allah, Buddha, or is it? What is this transformation? I don't have it.*

BORG: I like straightforward questions. I also think it's on to something really important. The Christian life—or the Buddhist life or the Muslim life, let's just say the religious life—isn't about trying to be good. It's not about trying to be bad, don't get me wrong, but it isn't about trying to be good. It is about a transformation of the self at a deeper level than that. Goodness is always better than badness, so don't misunderstand me there, but the notion that the Christian life is about trying to do something—trying to believe, trying to be good—is not the point. It's about the self at its deepest level. Borrowing from the 12 Steps, the Christian life is about letting go and letting God. That doesn't give you a recipe for how to do it, but it's about the transformation of the will and not primarily about the exertion of the conflicted will. And I think that transformation occurs.

The Christian life is about a relationship with God. If the word "God" sticks in your craw because you're not sure what I'm talking about, the Christian life is about our relationship to what is. By "what is," I don't mean the world of space, time, matter, and energy as understood by science. I mean something that's more mysterious than that. The way our relationship to God is nourished is through the very simple act, if you will, of paying attention to that relationship—there's nothing very mysterious about this. The analogy is to a human relationship. A human relationship grows and deepens to the extent that you pay attention to it, that you spend time in it. What we're talking about here is a transformation of the self that comes about through paying attention to our relationship with God. That can take so many forms. The most common form is prayer, and real close to it is worship, but it can also take the form of dream work, journaling, remembering God in the course of the day. All of that's involved in paying attention to the relationship. It's about practice, practice, practice. It's not about trying to be good—it's about seeking to become more and more centered in the reality that we name God.

Chapter 16

Listening for the Voice of God

THIS YEAR DURING THE SEASON of Epiphany, that season of the church year that immediately precedes the season of Lent, I was struck by the fact that Epiphany both begins and ends with stories from the Gospels in which we hear the voice of God. On the first Sunday in Epiphany we hear the story of the baptism of Jesus, with its climax in the voice of God speaking to Jesus: "You are my Son, the Beloved; with you I am well pleased" (Mark 1:11).

And then on the last Sunday in Epiphany, immediately before Ash Wednesday and the beginning of our Lenten

Sermon delivered at Calvary Episcopal Church, Memphis, Tennessee, as part of the Lenten Noonday Preaching Series, March 17, 2003.

journey, we hear the Transfiguration story, in which Jesus and the inner core of his disciples ascend to a high mountain. This time it is the disciples who hear the voice of God. The voice of God says, "This is my Son, the Beloved; listen to him" (9:7). The disciples, in a way, represent us in that passage. "Listen to him." Listen to Jesus.

This phenomenon of the divine voice actually has a name in the Jewish tradition. The Hebrew phrase that names this divine voice is *bat kol*. Let me translate that for you, because it's very interesting. Translated into English, *bat kol* literally means "the daughter of a sound." What kind of metaphor is this? The voice of God, the divine voice, is the daughter of a sound.

We hear this same voice in the Hebrew Bible in 1 Kings 19, the story of Elijah in a cave when the presence of God passes by him. We are told in the English translations of that story that Elijah hears a "still, small voice" (19:12, KJV)—that's the *bat kol*, "the daughter of a sound." The Hebrew for the voice that Elijah hears translates literally into English as a "sound of thinnest silence." So the daughter of a sound, the sound of thinnest silence, a still, small voice are all different ways of attempting to express what perhaps lies beyond the boundaries of speech.

Have you ever heard this voice? My wife was leading a Sunday morning group a couple of weeks ago in which she explained to the group this notion of the *bat kol*. After explaining it, she asked the group, "Have any of you ever heard this voice?" Several in the group had.

One woman spoke about a time when she was seven years old, and she heard a voice speak to her as clearly as any voice had ever spoken to her: "You belong to me." Then she said, "I didn't hear it with my ears. But I heard it."

Another woman reported an evening when she had an extraordinarily strong sense of the presence of Jesus in the room, and she said to Jesus, "Where have you been?" She heard a voice say back to her, "I never left you." She also said, "I didn't hear it with my ears. But I heard the voice."

It would be very interesting to ask you, "How many of you have heard such a voice?" I'm not going to ask for a show of hands, but it would be interesting to know that. Even if you've never heard such a voice, it's okay, because God also speaks to us in less dramatic ways.

We sometimes hear the voice of God in our dreams, if we know how to listen for it. We sometimes hear the voice of God in what our Quaker friends refer to as leadings or proddings, colloquially in "nudges and clobbers": if you don't get the nudge, you might get a clobber.

We sometimes hear the voice of God, again, in a less dramatic way in the events of our lives. The contemporary Christian writer Frederick Buechner has a wonderful way of putting this:

> Listen to your life. Listen to what happens to you, because it is through what happens to you that God speaks. It's in language that's not always easy to decipher, but it's there, powerfully, memorably, unforgettably.[1]

229

And so God speaks to us in the events of our lives.

Now, don't think that means that everything that happens to us is somehow God trying to get our attention. It doesn't mean that. It's more sacramental than that. Rather, in, with, and through the events of our lives, we are being addressed by God. God sometimes speaks to us through scripture, through that meditative devotional use of scripture that many of you are familiar with, perhaps, in a daily practice. God also speaks to us through the liturgical seasons of the church year. Indeed, that's one of their central purposes.

So we are back to the seasons of Epiphany and Lent and back to that *bat kol*—that voice that we hear in the Transfiguration story on the Sunday before the beginning of Lent. In that story, as I've already mentioned, the voice of God—the *bat kol*—speaks to the disciples, to us, and it says, "Listen to him." That is, listen to Jesus. Immediately after the Transfiguration story in Mark's Gospel—also in Matthew and Luke—immediately after that voice has said, "Listen to him," we get the story of Jesus's final journey from Galilee to Jerusalem.

The season of Lent is about accompanying Jesus on that journey, listening to Jesus as he journeys from Galilee to Jerusalem. On that journey Jesus speaks about the way—the path of following him. To listen to Jesus means to follow him on that path that leads to Jerusalem.

Jerusalem, in that story, is both the place of confrontation with a domination system and the place of death and resurrection, the place of endings and beginnings, of endings and new life, the place where what we feared was the place of death becomes the place of new life.

Listening to Jesus means embarking on that journey, and it is the journey at the very center of the Christian life. Jesus himself says, "If any want to become my followers, let them deny themselves and take up their cross and follow me" (Matt. 16:24). To follow Jesus is to follow the path of the cross. Paul says the same thing. Paul says, "I have been crucified with Christ; and it is no longer I who live, but it is Christ who lives in me" (Gal. 2:19–20).

To take the cross of Jesus seriously means to die with Christ and to be resurrected with Christ, to be reborn in Christ. Indeed, this is what is meant by that metaphor "to be born again." Listening to Jesus is about being born again. All of this together means dying to an old way of being and being born into a new way of being.

Dying to an old identity and being born into a new identity, an identity in God, in the Spirit, in Christ. This is what our Lenten journey is about. Indeed, in a sense, we're invited to do this every day—to die to that old way of being and be born into a new way of being.

In some ways, the heart of my sermon is: Why do we need this? Why do we need to die to an old way of being and be born into a new way of being?

It's because of something that happens to us very early in life, perhaps as early as infancy, and certainly by the time we are toddlers. It's something that happens in the preverbal stage of life, and what I'm speaking about here is the birth of self-awareness, the birth of self-consciousness, that awareness that the world is something separate from us.

If you're a newborn baby and you have excellent parents, it might take a while before the realization that the world is something separate from you emerges. If you're hungry, you get fed; if you're wet, you get changed; if you cry, you get picked up. But at some point, the world ceases to be immediately responsive to your needs, and you become aware that the world is something separate from you. That's the birth of self-consciousness or, even more simply, the birth of the separated self.

This is one of the central meanings of the Garden of Eden story, one of the central meanings of the Fall. The Fall isn't really about disobedience, though it's there in the story. The Fall is much more about the fact that we begin our lives, each of us individually, with a sense of undifferentiated union with what is. We begin our lives in paradise. But the birth of the separated self suddenly means we live our lives "east of Eden" in a state of separation and estrangement.

Let me use the best story I know for making this point, which I'm told is in one of the books of Parker Palmer. It's a story about a three-year-old girl who was the only child in her family. But now her mom is pregnant, and this three-year-old girl is very excited about having a baby in the house. The day comes when the mother-to-be is to deliver, and the mom and dad go off to the hospital. A couple of days later they come home with a new baby brother, and the little girl is just delighted.

After they've been home for a couple of hours, the little girl tells her parents that she wants to be with the baby in the baby's room, alone, with the door shut. She's absolutely insistent about the door being shut. Her folks find this unsettling. They know she's a good little girl, but they've also heard about sibling rivalry and all.

Then they remember that they've recently installed an intercom system in preparation for the arrival of the new baby. They realize that they can let their little girl do this, and if they hear the slightest weird thing happening, they can be in there in a flash.

So they let their little girl go into the room and close the door behind her. They race to the listening post. They hear her footsteps move across the room. They imagine her now standing over the baby's crib, and then they hear her say to her two-day-old baby brother, "Tell me about God. I've almost forgotten."

I find that to be a haunting and evocative story, because it suggests that we come from God, and when we are very, very young, we still remember that. We still know that. But the process of growing up, of learning the language of this world, is a process of progressive forgetting, in a sense, even a process of progressive obliterating of that memory. As we learn the language of this world, the categories of this world get imprinted upon our psyches, and our sense of being a separated self grows stronger and stronger. That sense of disconnection continues throughout childhood until, by the end of childhood, we may have lost that sense of connection altogether.

There's something about the very process of growing up that wounds us. We all grow up wounded. Our sense of separation increases through our adolescence as we continue to internalize all of the messages that we get from our culture about who we are and what we ought to be like.

Our sense of being a separated self with an identity conferred primarily by the values of our culture grows and grows. We have a sense of being okay or not okay to the extent that we measure up to these messages, and we often fall further into that world of separation and alienation, of comparison and judgment of self and others. The result is what the contemporary Benedictine teacher Thomas Keating calls "the false self," the self conferred by culture. Our identity is wrapped up in that false self. Or to refer to Frederick Buechner again:

> Increasingly, we live our lives from the outside in
> rather than from the inside out, taking our cues
> from the world, taking our cues from others,
> taking our cues from culture.

It is that way of being and that kind of identity that the Lenten journey calls us to die to. Listening to Jesus means undertaking this journey, embarking on that path of dying to the false self, to that identity, to that way of being, and to be born into an identity centered in Spirit, in Christ, in God. It is the process of internal redefinition of the self, so that a real person can be born within us.

We all know that Lent historically is a season of repentance. I don't know what your associations with repentance are, but mine from my childhood are pretty negative. Repentance means to feel really, really bad about the horrible person you are, to feel really, really bad because you've got impure thoughts—a big issue in adolescence. Repentance for me always kind of meant just feeling really, really sorry for being so disobedient to God.

The biblical meanings of repentance are much richer and much more important. To begin with, the Greek word for "repentance" that we find in the Gospels in the New Testament, is *metanoia*. Translating its Greek roots, "to repent" means "to go beyond the mind that you have," the mind that you have gotten from culture. From all of those messages, the identity you have is one that you've gotten from culture. To repent means to go beyond the mind that you have to a mind in Christ.

The meaning of the Hebrew word for "repentance" is also very rich. It's *shub* ("return"), and the home of this word in the Hebrew Bible is the Jewish experience of exile. To repent is to return. That's the meaning of the word. To return from exile, to return from that state of separation, to begin that journey of return from the separated self to a new self in God.

To repent is to reconnect with the one from whom we came and in whom we live and move and have our being. We do both—return and go beyond the mind that we have—by hearing the voice of God, which says to us: "Listen to him." Listen to Jesus. Listen to the way that he teaches, and follow him on this journey of Lent, with its climax in our participation in Good Friday and Easter, with its climax in our dying with Christ and being born again into life in God.

Afterword

FROM SECONDHAND TO FIRSTHAND RELIGION

by Barbara Brown Taylor

This eulogy was presented at the memorial service for Marcus J. Borg on March 22, 2015, at Trinity Episcopal Cathedral in Portland, Oregon.

And can any of you by worrying add a
single hour to your span of life? If then
you are not able to do so small a thing as
that, why do you worry about the rest?

Luke 12:25–26

WHY DO WE WORRY? What a silly question. We worry because we are able to imagine a future we cannot control. We worry because we are afraid of losing what we love. We know that worrying gets us nowhere, and still we cannot seem to stop. It's an ontological hazard, like thinning hair and bad knees. The sacred night is bearing down on us all, and there is not a single thing we can do about it. Why do we worry?

Because we are human, that's why.

Depending on where you live and whom you count on for spiritual guidance, you may have gotten the idea that faith and worry are incompatible. If you have the one, then you don't have the other. I see it on church signs all the time: "Worry Ends When Faith Begins," or "Worry Is the Devil's Data Plan—Don't Buy It." Maybe that message helps you. Or maybe it just proves that you don't have faith. Worst case, it can lead you to hide your worry in the presence of the faithful, pretending that you are just as tranquil as they all seem to be. In this way, too many of us become strangers to our own hearts.

Either Jesus's disciples did not know how to pretend—or they did know how and he saw right through them—because they were the people sitting right in front of him when he gave his "do not worry" speech. According to Luke, it wasn't a speech for the many, but for the few. It wasn't for those out on the edges of the crowd, but for those nearest the center. Jesus knew what was worrying them.

They didn't know where their next meal was coming from.

They didn't know whether their cloaks would be long enough to cover their feet that night when the dew fell and the bugs came out.

They didn't know how long they had to live—or him either.

They didn't know. That's what was worrying them. But instead of telling them to stop it, just stop—or letting them pretend they could stop—Jesus started doing the rabbi thing. He asked them what they did know—about the ravens and the lilies and the grass of the field. He asked them what they knew about God and God's kingdom. Most pointedly of all, he asked them what they knew about how well their worrying was working out for them. Were they feeling safer than before? Were they sleeping better at night? Had any of them gotten their "more life" rebates back in the mail yet?

At Piedmont College, this is what we call "engaging critical thinking," which does students a lot more good than a lecture and a fountain of free advice. Here's how it goes. A student starts worrying out loud about something he or she has learned in class, something that doesn't fit with an established belief. The teacher does not interrupt to argue or correct. He just waits until the student has gotten it all out and says, "Yes, I know you believe that. How's it working out for you? Yes, I know you're anxious. What kind of results are you getting from that?"

Jesus was that kind of teacher. Marcus Borg was too. He had compassion on the pretenders—those of us who led with what we had been taught to say and think about God, because it was how we had always earned our *A*s— but secondhand religion wasn't of much interest to him. Although he had a great gift for helping us rethink and respeak the faith, in the end it was our hearts he was after.

What mattered, he wrote in the book that brought him to the world's attention, was giving them away. That's how we make the move from secondhand to firsthand religion—from having heard about Jesus from the hearing of the ear to being in relationship with the living Christ. We do it by giving our hearts away.

Those were among his best words, written twenty years before the sacred night bore down on him. In those years Marcus poured himself into many books and talks, all seeking to move us from secondhand to firsthand religion—wisdom from a master who made the journey before us and wanted to offer help to those coming after. When the final night came, Marcus had yet another chance to move from the secondhand to the first—for who knows how well our best words will hold up under the reality of our own death?

Take Jesus's advice about considering the ravens and the lilies of the field. Does this really help? Ravens live twenty years at best; lilies, five to seven days. I hate to be the one to say it, but Jesus's assurance of divine care left some things to be desired. Longevity, for one thing. Protection, for another.

Marcus did not cling to those parts of the promise. When it became clear that longevity was no longer in the cards for him—and that his protection was going to look more like love than armor—he accepted the care that was left to him, both human and divine. By the accounts of those closest to him, during his last three months he experienced what can only be called a good death—and that only with a catch in the throat—but still. What a last, great gift from him, showing us what it looks like to (in his words) "die unto God and hope for the best."

So that is my stake in what we are doing today. Once we have given thanks for Marcus Borg's good life, what about the gifts of his good death? This is an early report, I know. Beatification can take years. But it's never too early to learn what we can from those who have gone before. Marcus's wife, Marianne, is my chief witness here, the one who told me how things went these last few months, so I hope you will hear the testimony of her whole family in the scraps I was able to gather up (yes—twelve baskets full).

Her first words to me were: "Marc died with such equanimity. He was not afraid. He had no pain. He did not gasp or grasp, though he had every reason to do both. His death was so economical—there was no excess, no drama. He was Scandinavian! It was real and it was hard, but once the threshold was in front of him, he crossed over it so quickly. He was always ahead of me, Barbara; I'm still catching up. My IQ has gone down 30 points since he died."

So there's one gift: no drama. This is easier, I think, for someone who has done what you might call "pre-hab." Almost thirty years ago, Marcus wrote about the importance of being mindful of one's own death. "People may need to be convinced that it's important," he said, but he was already there. He "worked out" with death before it was time, so he would have the strength he needed when the time came. In this, he stood in a long line of Christian sages. "Keep death daily before your eyes," St. Benedict wrote in his *Rule* in the middle of the sixth century. It's number 47 in his list of "instruments of good works," and it's not morbid. It's the key to abundant life.

Here's something else Marianne said about Marcus: "He had no unfinished business. There was no rancor in him for anyone; he did not waste his time on things like that." That's hard enough when all speak well of you, but when you have had quite a lot of rancor directed at you— well, there's a second gift. Most of the time I think people in the public eye are luckier than people who are not, because they have more opportunities to handle their egos. Marcus returned rancor with his own brand of Scandinavian cool. He debated his critics with such respect that they invited him out for drinks after. At home, in matters of the heart, he was all caught up.

The only thing he was working on when he died was his second novel, in which a character very much like Marcus was working through the death of his sister, who was very much like Marc's sister. Its tentative title was *Through a Glass Darkly*. "I don't know how it ends," he told Marianne, "but I want it to end on Thanksgiving."

As his lungs gave out, Marianne said, his body was (in the words of Mary Oliver) "a lion of courage." Against all odds, so was his sense of humor: a third gift. Apparently there was some mention of stuffing Marcus after he was gone, abandoned because he wasn't sure what his beloved pooch Henry would make of it. And never mind the T-shirts he had made up when Marianne became canon at

Trinity Cathedral ("Canon Without Balls"). I wasn't going to include that because I thought it might be inappropriate. But to laugh in the face of death is not necessarily to scoff; it may simply be a tip of the hat to the unbearable lightness of being.

Marianne didn't say this part, but the greatest gift of Marcus's good death for me was his willingness to trust God with insufficient information. "How do you know you're right?" someone asked him after a lecture. "I don't know," the wise man replied, pulling at his beard. "I don't know that I'm right." Does any of us, ever? Thank God Marcus told the truth.

During the last several months, Marianne said, she and Marcus leaned heavily on something William Sloane Coffin said when his son Alex died in a car wreck at the age of twenty-four. Ten days later, Coffin delivered Alex's eulogy at Riverside Church in New York City, where he was senior minister. Among many other things, he said this:

> In . . . my intense grief I felt some of my fellow reverends—not many, and none of you, thank God—were using comforting words of scripture for self-protection, to pretty up a situation whose bleakness they simply couldn't face. But like God herself, scripture is not around for anyone's protection, just for everyone's unending support. And that's what hundreds of you understood so beautifully. You gave me what God gives all of us—minimum protection, maximum support. I

swear to you, I wouldn't be standing here, were
I not upheld.

Minimum protection, maximum support. "Marc and I
held on to that," Marianne said, "even while we wondered
if it would turn out to be true."

"And?" I asked.

"So far, so good," she said.

If there isn't enough victory in that for some of us, there
is a surplus of truth in it for others—something to listen
for when the wind, the earthquake, and the fire have spent
themselves—when the sacred night bears down and the
sound of sheer silence is all that remains.

"So far, so good," she said.

"To die unto God and hope for the best," he said.

That's more than enough for a raven to live on, more
than enough to get a lily through the night. And for some
of us—when it is our turn to go—it is enough to help us
leave not as tearful slaves, but as kings and queens who
rise from the table with no further wants, having eaten
and drunk to the full.

Will we worry between now and then? Of course we
will. Why else did Jesus spend so much time doing pre-
hab with us? Because he knew pretenders when he saw
them, and what their pretending would do to their hearts.
Because he knew firsthand the weight of the sacred night.
Because he too worried about his life sometimes. And
still—once he got through with all the finger-wagging—
all the raven-praising and kingdom-coaching (was it one

of those sermons the preacher preaches because he needs to hear it himself?)—he met us right where we are today: "Do not be afraid."

How did you know?

Oh, little flock, it's written all over your faces.

Because Jesus said it, we take it on faith—until the time comes for each of us to discover firsthand if it's true. Or until, like Marcus, we make it true—by the way we live and by the way we die—and all for the love of God.

One last gift, from Marianne this time. "I'm so used to Marc being on the road," she said, "I kept expecting him to come home." She paused. "We were such a good match that I worried what I would do without his love. Then the other day while I was walking the kids (Henry and Abbey), I realized I still feel that love. I still have it—not in a sentimental way, but at a molecular level. You know how Jesus said, 'My peace I leave with you'? We've all heard it. Oh, I thought, so this is what that feels like." Firsthand.

Do not be afraid.

My peace I leave with you.

Come one, come all, and follow to the banquet hall.

Amen.

NOTES

CHAPTER 1: *Listening to the Spirit*

1. I believe that he was quoting or paraphrasing Karl Barth, though I am not aware whether it is published somewhere in Barth's writings or whether it is anecdotal.

2. See the excellent statement by Stanley Hauerwas and William Willimon in "Embarrassed by God's Presence," *Christian Century* (January 30, 1985): 98–100. They argue that both the modern church and modern theology are pervaded by the "practical atheism" of our time, that way of seeing and living that takes it for granted that there is no reality beyond the visible.

3. There are exceptions, to which I am indebted. Two studies from the last decade stand out: Geza Vermes, *Jesus the Jew* (New York: Macmillan, 1973), which treats the Jewish charismatic tradition contemporary with Jesus, and James D. G. Dunn, *Jesus and the Spirit* (Philadelphia: Westminster, 1975), a scholarly study of texts and traditions relevant to Jesus's relationship to the Spirit.

4. Of the many books that treat the subject of the modern worldview (or *Weltanschauung,* a German term that often appears even in books written in English), I have found two to be especially useful: W. T. Stace, *Religion and the Modern Mind* (Philadelphia: Lippincott, 1952), and Huston Smith, *Forgotten Truth: The Primordial Tradition* (New York: Harper & Row, 1976).

5. Though this is not the place to develop the point at length, the term "faith" has thus undergone a subtle but decisive shift in meaning in the modern period. For many people, faith now means "believing in the existence of God." In earlier times, it didn't take "faith" to believe *that* God existed—almost everybody took that for granted. Rather, "faith" had to do with one's *relationship* to God—whether one *trusted* in God. The difference between faith as "belief in something that may or may not exist" and faith as "trusting in God" is enormous. The first is a "matter of the head," the second a "matter of the heart"; the first can leave one unchanged, the second intrinsically brings change.

6. The phrase comes from Huston Smith, *Forgotten Truth;* see also his *Beyond the Post-Modern Mind* (New York: Crossroad, 1982). Other scholars have developed the same basic understanding, but I find

Smith's phrase "primordial tradition" as well as his exposition of the notion to be especially illuminating and helpful.

7. See, e.g., Mircea Eliade, *The Sacred and the Profane* (New York: Harcourt, Brace and World, 1959; originally published in French in 1956); and Rudolf Otto, *The Idea of the Holy* (New York: Oxford Univ. Press, 1958; first published in German in 1917). Otto introduced the term "numinous" as a way of speaking of the "holy," understood *not* as a moral term meaning righteous or pure but as a designation for the overpowering mystery (the *mysterium tremendum*) that is experienced in extraordinary moments.

8. In addition to the works by Smith, Eliade, and Otto already referred to, see William James's classic study *The Varieties of Religious Experience* (New York: Macmillan, 1961; originally published in 1902). James finds the origin of belief in an "unseen" world in the experience of "religious geniuses" who experience *firsthand* the realities of which religion speaks and carefully distinguishes this primal experience from what he calls "secondhand" religion, the beliefs that people acquire through tradition; see esp. 24–25, though the distinction remains important throughout his book.

9. To use Eliade's terms for a moment, the two worlds intersect in "theophanies" (manifestations of God) and "hierophanies" (manifestations of the holy). Otto speaks of experiences of the *numinous* (i.e., of the holy, or *numen,* a Latin term for "God"), which underlies phenomena.

10. For example, the temple at Delphi in Greece was seen as the "navel of the earth," the *axis mundi* connecting the two worlds; for other examples, see Eliade, *Sacred and Profane,* 32–47.

11. This is what the notion of God as creator has become in much of the modern world. Beginning with the deists of the seventeenth century, the concept of God began to function primarily as an intellectual hypothesis to account for the origin of everything. In cultural retrospect, this development may be seen as part of the process whereby Western intellectual culture weaned itself (or "fell," depending upon one's point of view) from a religious worldview to a secular worldview.

12. Neither the Old nor the New Testament uses abstractions such as omnipresence or transcendence, but the notion is clearly present. Classic Old Testament texts that point to the omnipresence of God are Ps. 139:7–10; 1 Kings 8:27; Isa. 6:3 ("the whole earth is full of his glory"). The notion of the immanent *Logos* at the beginning of John's Gospel points in the same direction, as do the words attributed approvingly by Luke to Paul in Acts 17:28: "In God we live and move and have our being." God is not "elsewhere"; we live in God.

13. See Smith, *Forgotten Truth*, 21: The "higher levels (of the primordial tradition) are not literally elsewhere; they are removed only in the sense of being inaccessible to ordinary consciousness." Or, to paraphrase William James in *The Varieties of Religious Experience*, we are separated from this other world only by the *filmiest screens of consciousness*; see esp. 305, 331, 335, 401.

14. For other experiences of the patriarchs involving contact with the other world, see, e.g., Gen. 12:7–9; 15:1–17; 17:1–2; 18:1–33; 26:23–25; 32:22–31.

15. The author of the book tells us that he received this vision while he was "in the Spirit" (1:10), presumably a state of nonordinary consciousness in which he momentarily "saw" into the other world. Revelation, part of the New Testament, is of course not in the *Hebrew* Bible, but it reflects the same worldview.

16. Though most of the Pentateuch concerns Moses, only a few chapters in the books of Kings speak of this ninth-century BCE prophet: 1 Kings 17–19, 21; 2 Kings 1–2.

17. Almost all of the Spirit-filled mediators mentioned in the Hebrew Bible are men. No doubt this is because the religion of ancient Israel was dominated by men. "Official" religious positions such as priest, prophet, and sage were restricted to men and, so far as we know, all of the biblical authors were men. Given this, it is noteworthy that the tradition does mention two charismatic women by name: Deborah the judge and Hulda the prophet. So also in other cultures dominated by patriarchy, though religious functionaries may have been male, the Spirit seems to show no gender preference.

18. For this whole section on Jewish "holy men" at the time of Jesus, see esp. Vermes, *Jesus the Jew*, 65–78, 206–13. Also relevant are E. E. Urbach, *The Sages* (Jerusalem: Magnes, 1975), 1:97–123; and, earlier, A. Büchler, *Types of Jewish Palestinian Piety* (New York: KTAV, 1968; first published in 1922), 87–107, 196–252.

19. From the Babylonian Talmud: *Taan.* 24b, *Ber.* 17b, *Hul.* 86a, all cited by Vermes, *Jesus the Jew*, 206. Vermes also notes that Rabbi Meir was called "Meir *my son.*"

20. From the Mishnah, *Taan.* 3.8, cited by Vermes, *Jesus the Jew*, 209.

21. Besides being known as people whose concentration in prayer was great and as mediators of divine power, they shared a number of other characteristics. Vermes notes that they were relatively detached from possessions, perhaps because the other world had a reality compared to which the preoccupations of this world seemed trivial. They were also suspected of being inadequately concerned about the laws of their tradition (like

many before and since whose awareness of the other realm is direct and experiential). Finally, though not restricted to Galilee, they seem to have been largely a Galilean phenomenon. Hanina, for example, was from a town in Galilee about ten miles from Nazareth.

22. See also 1 Cor. 12–14, where Paul speaks about the "gifts of the Spirit," some of which clearly involve direct relationship to the world of Spirit.

23. It is described three times in the book of Acts: 9:1–8; 22:6–11; 26:12–18.

24. In a poll I have taken in both university and church settings for about ten years, 90 percent of the participants regularly reply to stories of paranormal phenomena such as walking on burning coals in South Asia and Polynesia with, "It violates my sense of what is possible." Their sense of what is possible flows from the modern one-dimensional understanding of reality, in which everything must be explicable by chains of cause and effect within the material world, simply because that is the only world they see as "real."

25. Rudolf Bultmann's proposal for "demythologizing" the New Testament is a case in point. Recognizing that the New Testament writers often use the language of a three-story universe (heaven as "up," hell as "down," earth in the "middle"), Bultmann rightly stresses that such language is not to be taken literally (heaven is not really "up," and so forth). When the early Christians spoke of Jesus ascending into heaven or descending into hell, they could not have been describing a literal up-and-down motion through space. But, as Bultmann continues, it becomes clear that demythologizing involves not only a deliteralizing of the three-story universe, but also a collapse of the world of Spirit itself. That too does not conform to the modern worldview. See esp. his essay "New Testament and Mythology," in H. W. Bartsch, *Kerygma and Myth* (New York: Harper & Row, 1961; originally published in German in 1941), 1–16.

26. For a useful summary, see Smith, *Forgotten Truth,* 96–117. See also Ian Barbour, *Issues in Science and Religion* (New York: Harper & Row, 1971), 273–316; and Fritjof Capra, *The Tao of Physics* (Berkeley: Shambhala, 1975).

27. The historical and anthropological evidence is very strong. Not only are there frequent accounts of subjectively entering the other world, but paranormal happenings in this world are also reported. Paranormal healings are overwhelmingly attested in both the ancient and modern world. Clairvoyance is also quite well authenticated, and even something as bizarre as levitation is reasonably well grounded.

CHAPTER 4: *Jesus, Our Model for Being Spirit-Filled*

1. Two of the Gospels, Mark and John, say nothing at all about Jesus before his ministry, not even about his birth. Matthew and Luke do include accounts of his birth and early childhood, though in somewhat different form from each other (see Matt. 1–2; Luke 1–2). Moreover, the accounts contain many symbolic elements. Symbolic elements can be based on actual historical occurrence, but how much is historical we can no longer know. For a compact treatment of the birth stories, see W. Barnes Tatum, *In Quest of Jesus* (Atlanta: John Knox, 1982), 108–12; for a full treatment, see Raymond Brown's authoritative *The Birth of the Messiah* (Garden City, NY: Doubleday, 1977).

2. See Mark 6:3; Matt. 13:55; see also Geza Vermes, *Jesus the Jew* (New York: Macmillan, 1973), 21–22.

3. *Torah* in Hebrew means "divine teaching or instruction" and is most commonly translated "law." It has a range of meanings, sometimes referring to the first five books of the Bible (or Pentateuch), as in the phrase "the *law* and the prophets." It can also refer to the 613 specific written laws contained in the Pentateuch or, more broadly, to those laws plus the "oral law," which expands the written laws. To be trained in the Torah refers to being familiar with both the content of the law and the methods of interpretation and argumentation.

4. Included in the recitation were Deut. 6:4–9; 11:2–21; Num. 15:37–41.

5. The Essenes were a Jewish monastic group; see my *Jesus: A New Vision* (San Francisco: HarperSanFrancisco, 1987), 88.

6. According to Luke 3:23, he was "about thirty" when he began his ministry; according to John 8:57, Jesus was "not yet fifty." Though not being fifty is consistent with being about thirty, the former is an odd way of saying the latter. On other grounds, the younger age is to be preferred; the tradition that Jesus was born in the last years of Herod the Great (d. 4 BCE) is reasonably strong. Thus, at the beginning of his ministry, Jesus was probably in his early to middle thirties. Pilate was the Roman governor of Judea from 26 to 36 CE. Jesus was probably crucified in 30 CE, so his ministry probably began a year or a bit more before that.

7. The writings of Josephus are one of our primary sources for first-century Jewish history. As a young man, Josephus was a Jewish general in the great war against Rome, which broke out in 66 CE. Captured by the Romans in Galilee early in the war, he spent most of the rest of his life (perhaps another thirty-five years) in Rome, where he wrote his multivolume *Jewish Antiquities* and *History of the Jewish War* as well as two more minor works. Though Josephus refers to John the

Baptist, he apparently does not refer to the ministry of Jesus; the only direct reference is in a passage believed to be a Christian addition. The standard translation of Josephus is now the Loeb Classical Library edition, 9 vols., translated by H. St. J. Thackeray, R. Marcus, and A. Wikgrin (Cambridge: Harvard Univ. Press, 1958–65).

8. According to Mark 1:6, John wore "camel's hair" (presumably a camel skin) and a leather girdle; for a similar description of Elijah, see 2 Kings 1:8. For a "hairy coat" as the mark of a prophet, see Zech. 13:4. For John as prophet, see Mark 11:32; Matt. 11:9; Luke 7:26.

9. Ritual immersion in water (both in Judaism and other cultures) can have two different meanings. When repeated frequently (as it was among the Essenes), it has the meaning of a washing or purification. When it is a once-only ritual (as it apparently was for John), it may also be a purification, but its primary meaning is as an initiation ritual that symbolizes and confers a new identity. "Once-only" baptism was also known in Judaism; when a Gentile converted to Judaism, he or she was baptized (and if male, circumcised as well). But it is important to remember that John's baptism was intended for people who were already Jewish.

10. It is historically unlikely that John recognized Jesus at the time as an extraordinary or messianic figure. According to Mark, Luke, and Q ("Q" is a designation used by scholars to refer to material found in very similar form in *both* Matthew and Luke, but not in Mark; "Q" is thus presumed to be an early collection of traditions about Jesus that predates both Matthew and Luke and may be earlier even than Mark), there is no such recognition. The common image in Christian circles of John as primarily a forerunner of Jesus who self-consciously knew himself to be such and who recognized Jesus as "the coming one" is based on the Gospels of John and Matthew. According to John 1, the Baptist proclaims Jesus as the Lamb of God, Son of God, and even as one who preexisted him. But John's Gospel cannot be taken historically. Matt. 3:14 reports a snippet of conversation between Jesus and John; John says, "I need to be baptized by you, and do you come to me?" However, this (and Jesus's response) is almost certainly an insertion by Matthew into the story. Apart from these historically suspect references in John and Matthew, there is no reason to think that John believed Jesus to be "the coming one" at an early stage of the ministry. John's question from prison later in the ministry ("Are you the one who is to come, or are we to wait for another?" in Matt. 11:3 and Luke 7:19, and thus "Q" material) is therefore to be read as the dawning of curiosity or hope, not as the beginning of doubt.

11. According to Mark, the experience was private to Jesus. There is no indication that the crowd or John saw anything; and the "heavenly voice" in the next verse is addressed to Jesus alone ("You are . . ."). Matthew and Luke both change the text slightly, apparently making the experience of Jesus more public. According to Matthew, the voice declared Jesus's identity to the crowd (3:17); according to Luke, the Spirit descended in "bodily form" (3:22). The fact that Mark presents it as an internal experience of Jesus does not thereby make it less real.

12. See also Isa. 64:1 for the image of a "tear" or "rent" in the heavens: "O that you would *tear open* the heavens and come down . . ."

13. See *Jesus: A New Vision*, 31.

14. Such travel is found elsewhere in the Bible. Ezekiel, for example, reports, "The Spirit lifted me up between earth and heaven, and brought me in visions of God to Jerusalem" (8:3; see 11:1–2). For Elijah's travels "in the Spirit," see 1 Kings 18:12; cf. 2 Kings 2:11–12, 16. In the New Testament, see Acts 8:39–40. J. R. Michaels comments: "Jesus's journeys to the Holy City and to the high mountain belong in the same category as the journeys of Ezekiel" (*Servant and Son* [Atlanta: John Knox, 1981], 50). The phenomenon is widely reported in traditional cultures. See, e.g., John Neihardt, *Black Elk Speaks* (Lincoln: Univ. of Nebraska Press, 1961), and the books of Carlos Castaneda; even if Don Juan is regarded as a fictional character, as some have argued, his portrait is based on solid anthropological research. Such journeyings probably involve what are sometimes called "out-of-body" experiences.

15. Stephen Larsen, *The Shaman's Doorway* (New York: Harper & Row, 1976), 61–66. See also a section entitled "The Road of Trials" in Joseph Campbell, *Hero with a Thousand Faces* (Cleveland: World, 1956), 97–109. On shamanism more generally, see Mircea Eliade, *Shamanism: Archaic Techniques of Ecstasy* (New York: Pantheon, 1964); and W. A. Lessa and E. Z. Vogt, *Reader in Comparative Religion: An Anthropological Approach,* 3rd ed. (New York: Harper & Row, 1972), 381–412.

16. The vision at his baptism may well have been his "call story" (the Old Testament prophets apparently thought it important to tell such stories), and the temptation narrative seems to have a teaching function in addition to reporting an experience.

17. This occurs very frequently in the book of Acts, and the whole of the book of Revelation is presented as a series of visions.

18. The difference between communion with God and union with God is subtle and perhaps not important. Both are mystical states, and both are known in the Jewish-Christian tradition. In union with God, all sense of separateness (including the awareness of being a separate self)

momentarily disappears and one experiences only God; in communion with God, a sense of relationship remains. Communion is typically associated with Western mysticism and union with Eastern mysticism, though the contrast is not as sharp as the typical association suggests. See Peter Berger, ed., *The Other Side of God* (Garden City, NY: Anchor, 1981). For the "polarity" within Judaism, see esp. the essay by Michael Fishbane, "Israel and the Mothers," 28–47. For communion mysticism in the East, see the most popular form of Hinduism, *bhakti*.

19. From the Mishnah, *Ber.* 5.1; see A. Büchler, *Types of Jewish Palestinian Piety* (New York: KTAV, 1968; first published in 1922), 106–7.

20. For a history of Jewish mysticism reaching back to the time of Jesus and earlier, see esp. the work of Gershom Scholem, *Major Trends in Jewish Mysticism* (New York: Schocken, 1946), and *Jewish Gnosticism, Merkabah Mysticism, and Talmudic Tradition,* 2nd ed. (Hoboken: KTAV, 1965). A connection between apocalypticism and visions of or journeys into another world is increasingly affirmed in studies of Jewish apocalyptic. See, e.g., John J. Collins, *The Apocalyptic Imagination* (New York: Crossroad, 1984), which speaks of two strands of tradition in Jewish apocalypses, one visionary and one involving otherworldly journeys.

21. For an excellent summary of Jesus and prayer, including bibliography, see Donald Goergen, *The Mission and Ministry of Jesus* (Wilmington, DE: Michael Glazier, 1986), 129–45. Goergen's book arrived too late to be incorporated significantly into the present book, but I highly recommend it as one of the best recent works on the historical Jesus.

22. Luke emphasizes the role of prayer in Jesus's life more than the other evangelists do; in addition to 6:12, see 3:21; 5:16; 9:18; 9:28–29; 11:1. However, the picture is not due simply to Lucan redaction, as is clear from the references to Jesus's prayer life in the other Gospels.

23. Though this is the only occurrence of the Aramaic *Abba* in the Gospels (which were written in Greek), it may lie behind the unadorned "Father" in Luke's version of the Lord's Prayer (11:2). A consensus of scholarship affirms its authenticity. That it was also part of the prayer life of first-century Christians is indicated by the appearance of the word in Rom. 8:15 and Gal. 4:6, remarkable in letters composed in Greek for Greek-speaking audiences. It is reasonable to assume that early Christian usage derived from Jesus's own practice. The classic study of *Abba* is J. Jeremias, *The Prayers of Jesus* (Naperville, IL: Allenson, 1967), though Jeremias overemphasizes its distinctiveness, arguing that it was *unique* to Jesus (an argument perhaps motivated by theological considerations).

24. See Vermes, *Jesus the Jew*, 210–13.

25. Even by quite conservative scholars, Luke 4:18–30 is commonly attributed to Luke and categorized as "inauthentic" (i.e., not among the actual words of Jesus). To a large extent, this is because the placement of the sermon is so obviously the product of Luke's compositional work: these verses replace Mark's account of Jesus's "inaugural address" (Mark 1:15: "The kingdom of God has come near"). Moreover, the verses identify one of Luke's central themes: Luke stresses the presence of the Spirit in Jesus more than the other Gospels do. Thus it seems to be Luke's advance summary of who Jesus was and the thrust of his ministry. However, the possibility remains that Jesus did use these words with reference to himself at some other time in his ministry (perhaps even in the context of a synagogue reading—there is nothing improbable about the scene); though Luke is responsible for inserting the story at this point in the narrative, it is not necessarily created by Luke. Moreover, even if Luke did create the story, it aptly describes what we have seen to be true on other grounds. Whether Luke was reporting or creating tradition, he has seen well.

26. Rudolf Otto, *The Idea of the Holy* (New York: Oxford Univ. Press, 1958; first published in German in 1917), esp. 155–59. Otto writes, "The point is that the 'holy man' or the 'prophet' is from the outset, as regards the experience of the circle of his devotees, something more than a 'mere man.' He is the being of wonder and mystery, who somehow or other is felt to belong to the higher order of things, to the side of the numen itself. It is not that he himself teaches that he is such, but that he is *experienced* as such" (158, italics added). See also Otto's *The Kingdom of God and the Son of Man,* trans. F. V. Filson and B. L. Woolf (London: Lutterworth, 1938), esp. 162–69, 333–76.

27. As Otto puts it, in "these few masterly and pregnant words," Mark states "with supreme simplicity and force *the immediate impression of the numinous that issued from Jesus*" (*The Idea of the Holy,* 158; italics added).

28. On *Gevurah,* see E. E. Urbach, *The Sages* (Jerusalem: Magnes, 1975), 80–96; for his interpretation of this verse, see 85–86.

29. The Greek text means literally, "He is out of himself," that is, ecstatic, a nonordinary state often characteristic of holy men, easily mistaken as dementia.

30. The narrative, in which Jesus puts his opponents in a dilemma, is also an excellent example of Jesus's skillful repartee in debate.

31. Matthew has "Spirit of God" (12:28); Luke has "finger of God" (11:20); however, the two expressions are synonymous.

32. On "Amen," see Joachim Jeremias, *New Testament Theology* (New York: Scribner, 1971), 35–36. According to his tables, it appears thirteen times in Mark, nine times in Q, nine times in Matthew only, and three times in Luke, as well as twenty-five times in John. Thus all strata of the Gospel tradition attest to it.

33. See the six antithetical statements found in the Sermon on the Mount, Matt. 5:21–22, 27–28, 31–32, 33–34, 38–39, 43–44. Some scholars accept the antithetical formulation of only the first, second, and fourth as authentic (e.g., Rudolf Bultmann, *The History of the Synoptic Tradition* [New York: Harper & Row, 1963], 134–36). For a defense of the antithetical form as original to all six, see Jeremias, *New Testament Theology,* 251–53.

34. See also the call of Levi in Mark 2:13–14.

35. See Martin Hengel, *The Charismatic Leader and His Followers* (New York: Crossroad, 1981; originally published in German in 1968). Hengel finds Matt. 8:21–22 especially illuminating and notes that it echoes the call of Elisha by Elijah in 1 Kings 19:19–21.

36. For a superb and passionate exposition of prophetic consciousness (including the prophet as one who knew God), see Abraham Heschel, *The Prophets* (New York: Harper & Row, 1962), esp. vol. 1.

37. See also Matt. 17:1–8; Luke 9:28–36. Matthew calls the experience a vision.

38. Moses and Elijah are significant *not* because they represent "the law and the prophets," as is often stated in commentaries, for they were *not* symbolic of the law and prophets in the time of Jesus. Rather, they were the two great holy men of the Jewish scriptures.

39. See *Jesus: A New Vision,* 10–11.

40. For examples of it referring to Israel as a whole, see Hos. 11:1, Exod. 4:22–23; for examples referring to the king of Israel in particular, see Ps. 2:7, 2 Sam. 7:14.

41. This is an important point. To use a very mundane example, George Washington is legitimately referred to as "the father of his country" even though he presumably did not think of himself in those terms. Similarly, from a Christian point of view, Jesus is legitimately spoken of as the Messiah, *even if* he did not think of himself as such.

CHAPTER 5: *Reclaiming Mysticism*

1. Stephen Larsen, *The Shaman's Doorway* (New York: Harper & Row, 1976), 66.

2. One of the most comprehensive and yet compact descriptions of mystical experience is William James, *The Varieties of Religious Experience*

(New York: Macmillan, 1961; originally published in 1902), 299–336, esp. 299–301. James stresses the *noetic* quality, as does the title of Andrew Greeley's *Ecstasy: A Way of Knowing* (Englewood Cliffs, NJ: Prentice-Hall, 1974).

3. The difference between union and communion mysticism is difficult to explain. In mystical experience, the subject-object distinction of ordinary awareness disappears. For union mystics, everything becomes subject or, perhaps more accurately, everything becomes one (or "not two") beyond the subject-object distinction. For communion mystics, the subject-object distinction disappears, but it is not replaced by undifferentiated oneness. Instead, what might be called a subject-subject relationship emerges: knowing and being known by.

4. Called "Galilean charismatics" in Geza Vermes, *Jesus the Jew* (New York: Macmillan, 1973), 206–13.

5. Gershom Scholem, *Jewish Gnosticism, Merkabah Mysticism, and Talmudic Tradition,* 2nd ed. (New York: Jewish Theological Seminary of America, 1965), 23–27.

6. Gershom Scholem, *Major Trends in Jewish Mysticism* (New York: Schocken, 1961), 40–79. In addition to dating Jewish mysticism prior to the current era, Scholem notes its connection to apocalyptic thought (40–43, 73) and Pharisaic circles (41–42), its use of fasting and special postures of prayer (49–50), and its association with miraculous powers (50–51). David Suter connects the parables of Enoch, which he dates in the middle first century CE, to the Hekhaloth tradition (*Tradition and Composition in the Parables of Enoch* [Atlanta: Society of Biblical Literature, 1979], 14–23). Martin Hengel traces the special revelations of Hasidic apocalyptic to mystical experiences (*Jews, Greeks and Barbarians* [Philadelphia: Fortress, 1980], 124). See also Hengel, *Judaism and Hellenism* (Eugene, OR: Wipf and Stock, 1974), 1:207. Jacob Neusner approvingly reports M. Smith's claim that mystical elements developed within Judaism in the pre-Christian Hellenistic period (*Early Rabbinic Judaism* [Leiden: Brill, 1975], 142) and notes that we must suppose that Jewish gnosticism existed prior to 70 CE (148).

7. See Abraham Heschel's exposition of *daath elohim,* "knowing God," in *The Prophets,* vol. 1 (New York: Harper & Row, 1969), 57–60. Though Heschel avoids using the term "mysticism" in this context, *daath elohim* is a *direct* knowing *of* God, not a knowing *about* God.

8. The term may also lie behind the unadorned "father" in Luke's version of the Lord's Prayer (11:2). That it was an important part of the prayer life of first-century Christians is indicated by its appearance in Rom. 8:15 and Gal. 4:6, documents composed in Greek for Greek-speaking

audiences. It is reasonable to conclude that early Christian usage derived from Jesus's own use of the term. The classic study is Joachim Jeremias, *The Prayers of Jesus* (Naperville, IL: Allenson, 1967), though he overstates the case for uniqueness. For parallels in texts about Jewish Spirit persons, see Vermes, *Jesus the Jew,* 210–13.

9. "Q" is a designation used by scholars to refer to material found in very similar form in *both* Matthew and Luke, but not in Mark; "Q" is thus presumed to be an early collection of traditions about Jesus that predates both Matthew and Luke and may be earlier even than Mark.

10. Though the saying's credentials as Q material are excellent, scholars tend to attribute it to the early Christian community instead of to Jesus, reading it as asserting the unique sonship of Jesus, a conviction clearly held by the post-Easter community. For a rehearsal of the arguments for and against authenticity, see James D. G. Dunn, *Jesus and the Spirit* (Philadelphia: Westminster, 1975), 27–34. Yet its language and content are at home in a pre-Easter Palestinian milieu (see esp. Joachim Jeremias, *New Testament Theology* [New York: Scribner, 1971], 56–61); and other Jewish charismatic men spoke of themselves as "son" in a sense that distinguished them from other Jews who were also called "sons" (see Vermes, *Jesus the Jew,* 209).

11. Jeremias, *New Testament Theology,* 58.

12. See, e.g., Ps. 139:1–18.

13. See my *Conflict, Holiness, and Politics in the Teachings of Jesus* (Harrisburg, PA: Trinity, 1984), 188–89. Further evidence for the Jesus movement's attitudes may be found in the Lucan infancy hymns, which are likely to have had their *Sitz im Leben der alten Kirche* in the Palestinian church and understand peace for Israel to be among the potential consequences of Jesus's advent (Luke 1:79; 2:14). See H. L. MacNeill, "The *Sitz im Leben* of Lk. 1:5–2:20," *Journal of Biblical Literature* 65 (1946): 123–30; Lloyd Gaston, *No Stone on Another* (Boston: Brill Academic, 1970), 256–76. That they have their origin in a Palestinian community does not depend on a linguistic argument for a Semitic origin; i.e., if one affirms with H. F. D. Sparks that the Semitisms are explicable as Lucan "Septuagintalisms," this does not entail the view that the hymns are Lucan creations ("The Semitisms of St. Luke's Gospel," *Journal of Theological Studies* 44 [1943]: 129–38). Indeed, Sparks himself affirms that they are probably based on earlier tradition (135–36). Also affirming a Christian community origin for the hymns (as opposed to a Baptist or Lucan origin) are, among others, Walter Wink, *John the Baptist in the Gospel Tradition* (Cambridge: Cambridge Univ. Press, 1968), 60–72; D. Jones, "The

Background and Character of the Lukan Psalms," *Journal of Theological Studies* 19 (1968): 19–50.

14. It seems that often what Jesus meant by it is determined on the basis of whether or not it can make sense as public policy in all periods of history. Since this would, it is argued, often involve the suffering of innocents against whom unjust aggression had occurred, it cannot be intended as public policy, but only for the Christian's personal behavior, when he or she *alone* takes the consequences. For a statement of the dilemma, see James Wood, *The Sermon on the Mount and Its Application* (London: Geoffrey Bles, 1963), 96–108. Whatever one says about its permanent application, one can say that, historically considered, it was intended as a collective posture at a particular time in history toward a particular state.

15. See T. W. Manson, *Servant-Messiah* (Cambridge: Cambridge Univ. Press, 1953), 70–71; Josef Blinzler, "Die Niedermetzelung von Galiläern durch Pilatus," *Novum Testamentum* 2, no. 1 (1957): 43–47; H. Montefiore, "Revolt in the Desert? Mark 6:30ff.," *New Testament Studies* 8 (1961–62): 135–41; C. H. Dodd, *Historical Tradition in the Fourth Gospel* (Cambridge: Cambridge Univ. Press, 1963), 212–17, and *Founder of Christianity* (New York: Macmillan, 1970), 131–34.

16. It does not answer the broader question of what is the emperor's and what is God's. Moreover, it is inadequate as a basis for describing the politics of Jesus, as if this were the central political pronouncement of his ministry. The thrust of this study is that there is so much more that must be included under the "politics of Jesus."

17. *Contra* J. Spencer Kennard (*Render to God* [New York: Oxford Univ. Press, 1950], passim) and S. G. F. Brandon (*Jesus and the Zealots* [New York: Scribner, 1967], 345–49), both of whom argue that "Give to God the things that are God's" would have been understood to prohibit payment of tax to the emperor, since the wealth of the Holy Land was God's, not the emperor's. Yet in the context of handling a coin of the emperor's, "Give to the emperor" must surely mean, "Go ahead and pay it." See also, among others, Ethelbert Stauffer, *Christ and the Caesars* (Philadelphia: Westminster, 1955), 112–37; W. L. Knox, "Church and State in the New Testament," *Journal of Roman Studies* 39 (1949): 23; M. Rist, "Caesar or God (Mark 12:13–17)? A Study in Formgeschichte," *Journal of Religion* 16 (1936): 317–31; J. Duncan and M. Derrett, *Law in the New Testament* (London: Darton, Longman & Todd, 1970), 34–37. For research and bibliography, see C. H. Giblin, "'The Things of God' in the Question Concerning Tribute to Caesar," *Catholic Biblical Quarterly* 33 (1971): 510–14.

18. See Mark 10:42–43 and parallels; cf. Luke 22:25–26.

19. On "fox," see Harold Hoehner, *Herod Antipas* (Cambridge: Cambridge Univ. Press, 1972), 220–21, 343–47.

20. The recognition that Jesus's message of repentance did not involve a turning from individual sins to individual virtues, but rather included national shortcomings, helps to explain the frequently cited problem of why Paul and other New Testament letter writers do not more often invoke the moral authority of Jesus when offering ethical instruction. The problem, identified by David L. Dungan (*The Sayings of Jesus in the Churches of Paul* [Philadelphia: Fortress, 1971], xvii–xxix, with citation of literature), is largely resolved by the recognition that the specific ethical teaching of Jesus did not consist of generalized morality or universally applicable laws for living, but concerned the specific politico-religious crisis of Israel. What he did say was often so related to the particularities of the Palestinian crisis that it could be used in another milieu only by modification and transformation, a process that by no means needs to be viewed as illegitimate.

21. See also Gerd Theissen, *Sociology of Early Palestinian Christianity* (Philadelphia: Fortress, 1978), 77–87.

22. R. C. Dentan, *Interpreter's Dictionary of the Bible,* ed. G. A. Buttrick (New York: Abingdon, 1962), 2:549.

23. William D. Davies, *Paul and Rabbinic Judaism,* 3rd ed. (London: SPCK, 1970), 20–35; E. E. Urbach, *The Sages* (Jerusalem: Magnes, 1975), 471–83.

24. Urbach, *The Sages,* 473.

25. See also Luke 14:26–27; Matt. 10:37–38; and the closely related images of "drinking the cup" and being baptized with Jesus's baptism in Mark 10:38.

26. Presumably Luke added "daily" when he incorporated Mark's text into his Gospel.

27. The image seems closely related to the Johannine emphasis on being born again; see John 3:1–8.

28. On two occasions, the context is self-exaltation through religious status: Luke 18:14, the parable of the Pharisee and the tax collector; Matt. 23:12, the honor enjoyed by religious teachers. On another occasion, the context is self-exaltation through social (or religious?) status as indicated by the seating arrangements at a banquet (Luke 14:7–11). The other context is teaching on greatness (Matt. 18:1–4).

29. See, e.g., G. E. Mendenhall, *Interpreter's Dictionary of the Bible,* 2:659.

30. Cf. Phil. 2:5–11, where *"emptied* himself, taking the form of a slave," is parallel to "he *humbled* himself and became obedient to the point

of death." Many scholars have argued that these words are from a pre-Pauline hymn, suggesting a very early Christian tradition. In addition to the parallel between self-emptying and humbling, note the connection of both to *servant/slave* and *death.*

31. See, e.g., Rom. 6:1–11; see esp. v. 3: "all of us."

32. Following the opening verse of the Gospel, which is really the title, Mark begins his Gospel with a Hebrew Bible quotation suggesting that his Gospel concerns "the way." Each of the three occasions on which Jesus speaks of his impending death in Mark 8–10 is followed immediately by teaching directed to his followers concerning the way of death (8:31–35; 9:30–35; 10:32–40). The Gospel climaxes in the death of Jesus, which is understood as opening up access to the presence of God (15:38); i.e., the way into the presence of God is through death. That Mark's Gospel may be used cautiously as evidence for the Jesus movement's understanding flows out of the growing tendency among scholars to locate the composition of Mark's Gospel in Syria, part of the area included within the Jesus movement's activity; see, e.g., Howard C. Kee, *Community of the New Age: Studies in Mark's Gospel* (Philadelphia: Westminster, 1977), 100–105, esp. 105, where Kee speaks of "rural and small-town southern Syria."

33. Whether this may be used as evidence for the Jesus movement's point of view depends upon how one views the tradition that Luke received. Is the "journey toward death" section a Lucan composition or was it already present in "proto-Luke"? For an extended argument that the pre-Lucan traditions reflect the missionary activity of the Palestinian church (the Jesus movement), see Gaston, *No Stone,* 244–369.

34. According to I. M. Lewis, "The shaman's initial crisis represents the healer's passion, or, as the Akawaio Indians themselves put it, 'a man must die before he becomes a shaman'" (*Ecstatic Religion: An Anthropological Study of Spirit Possession and Shamanism* [Harmondsworth, England: Penguin, 1971], 70).

35. On the connection between the forms of Jesus's teaching and the "end of world," see esp. the work of William Beardslee and John Crossan, compactly reported in Norman Perrin, *Jesus and the Language of the Kingdom* (Philadelphia: Fortress, 1976), 48–56.

36. Theissen, *Sociology of Early Palestinian Christianity,* 104–5; see also 79–80, 103–7.

37. Theissen recognizes the connection between the particularities of the historical situation and this aspect of Jesus's teaching. He notes that though it "certainly points far beyond the particular historical context in which it came into being," it was initially "a contribution toward

overcoming a deep-rooted crisis in Judaism" (*Sociology of Early Palestinian Christianity,* 107).

CHAPTER 6: *Awe, Wonder, and Jesus*

1. For an excellent introduction to the modern scholarly treatment of the miracle stories, see R. H. Fuller, *Interpreting the Miracles* (Philadelphia: Westminster, 1963). Somewhat more technical studies include D. L. Tiede, *The Charismatic Figure as Miracle Worker* (SBL Dissertation Series 1, 1972); H. C. Kee, *Miracle and the Early Christian World: A Study in Socio-Historical Method* (New Haven, CT: Yale Univ. Press, 1983); G. Theissen, *The Miracle Stories of the Early Christian Tradition* (Philadelphia: Fortress, 1983).

2. John's question, "Are you the one who is to come?" did not inquire if Jesus were the Messiah, as is sometimes thought. Instead, the phrase "the one who is to come" is explicitly associated with the expectation of Elijah (see Mal. 3:1; 4:5), not the Messiah.

3. For example, no less than two-thirds of Mark's Gospel prior to the story of Jesus's last week in Jerusalem concerns the miraculous.

4. Matthew 12:27 (Luke 11:19); Mark 9:38–39; 6:7–13; 9:18; Matt. 10:1–8; Luke 9:1–6; 10:17.

5. For studies of possession and exorcism, see I. M. Lewis, *Ecstatic Religion: An Anthropological Study of Spirit Possession and Shamanism* (Harmondsworth, UK: Penguin, 1971).

6. See, for example, an account of a Jewish exorcist roughly contemporary with Jesus: "Eleazar put to the nose of the possessed man a ring which had under its seal one of the roots prescribed by Solomon, and then, as the man smelled it, drew out the demon through his nostrils, and, when the man at once fell down, adjured the demon never to come back into him, speaking Solomon's name and reciting the incantations which he had composed." The episode is reported in Josephus, *Jewish Antiquities* 8:46–48.

7. The story contains many details that point to a symbolic meaning as well. The picture Mark paints in his narrative is full of images of impurity or "uncleanness," which was believed to separate one from "the holy" (God). The demoniac lived in Gentile ("unclean") territory; he also lived among tombs (proximity to death was seen as one of the most powerful sources of defilement); he lived near pigs, which were an "unclean" animal; and he was possessed by an "unclean spirit." The scene is a picture of all that separated one from God within the framework of the religious beliefs of the time. The story makes the point that Jesus is one who overcomes the most potent and devastating sources

of defilement and alienation, banishes the forces of evil from life, and restores their victims to both health and human community (the exorcism ends with the demoniac "clothed and in his right mind" and told to "go home").

8. The description of a seizure in this episode should not lead to an equation between possession and epilepsy; they are two quite different phenomena.

9. The location of the story in the Gospel narrative shows the importance of Jesus's exorcisms to Mark; this is the first *public event* of Jesus's ministry reported by Mark, following immediately upon Jesus's gathering of the nucleus of the disciples.

10. For *Gevurah* as the "mouth of power" or Spirit, see E. E. Urbach, *The Sages* (Jerusalem: Magnes, 1975), 80–96; for his interpretation of this verse, see 85–86.

11. See the provocative and illuminating discussion by M. Scott Peck in *People of the Lie* (New York: Simon & Schuster, 1983), 182–211. Peck, a practicing psychiatrist, began his study of possession and exorcism believing that a clinical diagnosis within the framework of current psychological understanding would be possible. However, he and a team of professionals eventually became involved in two cases of "possession" (and exorcism) that he could not account for within a purely psychological framework.

12. See esp. Lewis, *Ecstatic Religion*.

13. For a very illuminating description of the cosmology of such societies, see Mary Douglas, *Natural Symbols: Explorations in Cosmology* (New York: Pantheon, 1970), viii–ix, 103, 107–24.

14. For the complete account, see Mark 3:22–30; Matt. 12:22–37; Luke 11:14–23. Beelzebul is a name for Satan; its two variants, Beelzebul and Beelzebub, mean "lord of dung," "lord of flies."

15. In societies that affirm possession and exorcism, accusations of witchcraft are commonly used "to express aggression between rivals and enemies" (Lewis, *Ecstatic Religion,* 33). For the rivalry between Jesus and his opponents as involving accusations of witchcraft, see Jerome Neyrey and Bruce Malina, *Calling Jesus Names* (Sonoma, CA: Polebridge, 1988), chap. 1.

16. From the Babylonian Talmud, *Sanh.* 43a.

17. The word "magician" is not used in its modern sense of an entertainer who performs magic tricks. Rather, it is used in its ancient sense of one who can manipulate the powers of the spirit world. See esp. the works of Morton Smith: *Jesus the Magician* (San Francisco: Harper & Row, 1978) and his earlier *Clement of Alexandria and a Secret Gospel*

of Mark (Cambridge: Harvard Univ. Press, 1973). Smith basically affirms the perspective of Jesus's opponents, amassing a great amount of evidence concerning magical practices in the ancient world as he does so. Walter Wink's critical and yet appreciative review of Smith's first volume is appropriate as an assessment of both. One senses, Wink writes, "subliminally that Smith's interest is in discrediting Christianity through a debunking of Jesus," and yet part of Smith's work is "a stunning scholarly achievement. . . . The great value of Smith's discussion of Jesus's 'magic' is that he does place Jesus's healings and exorcisms within a broader context of first-century 'magical' practices hitherto largely ignored" ("Jesus as Magician," *Union Seminary Quarterly Review* 30 [1974]: 3–14; quotes from 9–10).

18. For example, Mark 1:34: "He cured many who were sick with various diseases"; 3:9–10: "And he told his disciples to have a boat ready for him because of the crowd, so that they would not crush him; for he had cured many, so that all who had diseases pressed upon him to touch him."

19. The list of *types* of healings (the blind see, deaf hear, lame walk, and so forth) is largely drawn from Old Testament passages that refer to the coming age (which is also referred to as the outpouring of the Spirit). Thus it is not clear whether the list was meant to be a citation of the categories of Jesus's actual healings, or whether it was a way of saying that the coming age (the outpouring of the Spirit) had begun.

20. See also Mark 8:22–26, which reports that Jesus applied spit to the eyes of a blind man.

21. In the story of the catch of fish (Luke 5:1–11), Jesus functions as "game finder" for his fishermen disciples, even though that is not the point of the story (the point of the story is that the disciples are now to become "fishers of men"). One of the traditional functions of holy men in hunting and fishing societies is game finding; that is, they use their powers for the sake of "the tribe" (their people). In agricultural societies, the parallel function is rainmaking. The story of the cursing of the fig tree (Mark 11:12–14, 20–25) is especially perplexing because it seems "out of character." Scholars have often speculated that the story may have grown out of a parable about a fig tree that Jesus told (Luke 13:6–9). In any case, Mark's placement of the fig-tree narrative suggests a symbolic meaning. The story is told in two parts, with the "cleansing of the Temple" separating the two halves. Mark apparently sees a connection between the fig tree (which is sometimes an image for Israel) having no fruit on it and the Temple not serving the purpose for which it was intended. The "withering" of the fig tree points to the future awaiting Jerusalem and the Temple.

22. This is a different question from the question, "Are there limits to the power of God?" Our question is whether the mediation of that power through human beings is limited in any way. Illustrative here is the story of a Christian saint, St. Denis, who as bishop of Paris was martyred by the Romans in the third century. After his beheading, we are told, he picked up his severed head and walked several miles to his church where, still holding his severed head under his arm, he sang the Mass. Do things like that happen? "With God all things are possible," one might say. But does that mean all things are possible to or through a Spirit-filled mediator? To express historical skepticism about such accounts does not imply doubting the power of God.

23. The recognition that some of the miracle stories may be *wholly symbolic* and not historical is usually credited to David Friedrich Strauss, whose two-volume *Life of Jesus* was published in 1835 when Strauss was only twenty-seven. Prior to Strauss, scholars generally agreed that the miracle stories were to be read as *historical* narratives and differed on the question of whether a supernatural or natural explanation of the story was to be sought. An example of a "natural explanation" offered by one of Strauss's contemporaries (and which I once heard in a sermon) argues that the feeding of the five thousand is to be explained as follows. Many in the crowd actually had brought food, and the action of the boy in "sharing" his five loaves and two fishes moved the rest of the crowd to act in a similarly generous fashion. Ironically, the explanation preserves the "happenedness" of the story, but destroys the miracle. Strauss cut through this preoccupation with treating the miracle stories as historical and suggested instead that many of the miracle stories are to be understood as literary creations of the early church that draw upon the rich imagery of the Old Testament: their meaning lies in their symbolism. Strauss's book was radical in his day; a review called it the most pestilential book ever vomited out of the bowels of hell, and he was blackballed from the universities of Europe. With modification, his approach has now become the position of mainstream scholarship.

24. For the nonhistorical character of John, see *Jesus: A New Vision,* 4–6.

25. The same theme appears in the longer ending to Mark's Gospel, added some time in the second century, which almost certainly does not report actual words of Jesus, but does report what some early Christians believed he had said to his followers: "They will pick up snakes in their hands, and if they drink any deadly thing, it will not hurt them" (Mark 16:18; in the judgment of most scholars, Mark's Gospel originally ended with 16:8). This verse is taken literally by a few Christians and is the

scriptural basis for handling poisonous snakes in the context of Christian worship.

26. From the Jerusalem Talmud, *Ber.* 9a. Also reported in the Babylonian Talmud, *Ber.* 33a, and the Tosefta, *Ber.* 2.20.

27. For an excellent discussion of the relationship between faith and historical judgment, see Van Harvey, *The Historian and the Believer* (New York: Macmillan, 1966).

28. Fuller, *Interpreting the Miracles,* 38.

CHAPTER 10: *Renewing Our Image of Jesus*

1. Walter Brueggemann, *The Prophetic Imagination* (Philadelphia: Fortress, 1978).

2. Gerd Theissen, *Sociology of Early Palestinian Christianity* (Philadelphia: Fortress, 1978).

3. See Huston Smith's *Forgotten Truth: The Primordial Tradition* (New York: Harper & Row, 1976), in which he sketches the multidimensional model of reality and the self that he finds to be virtually a cultural universal, attested to by the collective experience of humankind prior to the modern period.

CHAPTER 13: *Facing Today's Challenges*

1. *Putting Away Childish Things* (San Francisco: HarperOne, 2010).

CHAPTER 16: *Listening for the Voice of God*

1. Frederick Buechner, *Listening to Your Life: Daily Meditations with Frederick Buechner* (San Francisco: HarperSanFrancisco, 1992).

SCRIPTURE INDEX

Bold numbers refer to chapter and verse.

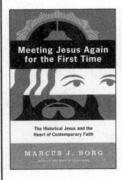